A 1960s
East End
Childhood

A 1960s
East End
Childhood

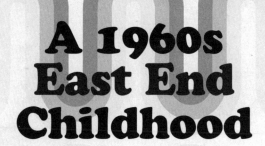

Simon Webb

The
History
Press

The author (right) and his sister enjoy playing in the snow in 1962.

First published 2012

The History Press
The Mill, Brimscombe Port
Stroud, Gloucestershire, GL5 2QG
www.thehistorypress.co.uk

© Simon Webb, 2012

The right of Simon Webb to be identified as the Author
of this work has been asserted in accordance with the
Copyrights, Designs and Patents Act 1988.

British Library Cataloguing in Publication Data.
A catalogue record for this book is available from the British Library.

ISBN 978 0 7524 7484 7

Typesetting and origination by The History Press
Printed in Great Britain
Manufacturing managed by Jellyfish Print Solutions Ltd

Contents

Visitors to London await the Changing of the Guard at Buckingham Palace, 1962. (Don O'Brien)

Introduction

There is, and always has been, a temptation for older people to claim that the world was a lot better when they were young themselves. This is nothing new. Over two thousand years ago, the prophet Ecclesiastes said, 'Never ask, "Oh why were things so much better in the old days?" It's not an intelligent question.'

As a child who grew up in East London during the 1950s and '60s, I have, in recent years, been fascinated to see how perceptions have changed; childhood, during that time, becoming transformed into some sort of golden age to be remembered with aching nostalgia and affection. The idea seems to be that children were far healthier and happier in those days – playing outdoors all day with no fear of muggers and child molesters, or worries about traffic. How many times have we read the wistful reminiscences of middle-aged men and women who, as children, left the house in the morning and didn't come back until they were hungry? Apparently, nowhere was this happy state of affairs more prevalent than in the East End of London. Life was, at least according to some recent accounts, one long round of playing hopscotch in the streets and larking around on bombsites. In this book, I shall be looking objectively at a world which I remember very clearly, and just to be on the safe side, I shall also be checking my own memory against contemporary records and statistics.

This book will be a 'warts and all' portrait of that particular childhood era, removing the rose-tinted spectacles sometimes used to view the past, but the reality of life fifty years ago in East London is actually far more interesting and complex than one would guess from first glance. To give one small example; the notion that children in the 1960s played happily and safely in the streets because there was so much less traffic than there is today. This particular part of the mythology of childhood in the old East End is so very

Fasset Square, the model for Albert Square in *EastEnders*.

much at odds with my own recollections, that I thought it worth exploring the matter in depth, making use of official figures rather than relying upon my own memories or those of my contemporaries. The results of this investigation are surprising – one might almost say shocking.

In fact, despite there being so few vehicles, ten times as many children died on the roads in 1961 as were killed in road accidents in 2010. A disproportionate number of these deaths occurred in working-class areas such as the East End. The same is true of all other types of accidental death in childhood; the further back one goes, the more children were killed each year. Not only were far more children being killed and injured by accidents and all other causes fifty years ago, those living in deprived, working-class districts like the East End were very much more likely to suffer harm. Children from social groups four and five – the sons and daughters of manual workers – were many times more likely to be killed by cars, fires and other accidents than those from social class one – those with professional and managerial parents.

This association between family income and childhood death continues today. Children from single-parent families are twice as likely to die in road accidents as those living with both parents. Even more shocking is the fact that children today whose parents have never worked are thirty-seven times more likely to die in house-fires than those whose parents are professionals.

Moving away from accidental injuries and deaths, another statistic from that time that gives us pause for thought is the infant mortality rate. This rate, the percentage of babies dying before their first birthday in East London in 1960, was the same then as in a present-day, third-world country like Egypt.

The truth is, life for children in East London fifty years ago was very much more risky than it is for children in the area now. The hazardous nature of childhood in the East End of the 1960s is real in my own memory. One reads frequently of kids playing hopscotch on the pavement in those days, but seldom about 'Last One Across'; a game in which a group of boys would race across a busy road or railway line, the winner being the last to clear the path of the oncoming traffic or train. This game, popular among the livelier children in that part of London, caused many injuries and some deaths. Similarly, airguns and catapults were commonly carried. Such things are all very well in the pages of a *Just William* book, but in real life both are quite capable of taking out somebody's eye. I knew two people at school who had lost eyes in this way. Fireworks were also readily available and regularly misused. One youth a couple of years above me at school, gathered dozens of bangers together and constructed a bomb from them. The fuse seemed to have gone out; he went back to investigate and the thing exploded, blowing off his hand.

This book is not intended to be, in any way, an exercise in demythologising or debunking, rather it is hoped that it will give a more rounded and balanced portrait of children's lives in the East End of half a century ago. There was much that was good about childhood in those days, but also a good deal that was not. I shall be doing my best to show all aspects of childhood at that time, with the highlights as well as the less savoury aspects.

Simon Webb, 2012

1

The East End in 1960

We begin in a world which, although only separated by fifty years from our own, is almost wholly unrecognisable. It is a world of steam trains and trolley buses; a world where practically everybody smokes all the time, even in doctor's waiting rooms or hospital wards. Murderers are still being hanged and you would be hard pressed to spot a black face anywhere in the country outside one or two urban ghettoes, such as Notting Hill or Brixton. There are only two channels on television, both black and white, and the majority of British films showing at the cinema are also in black and white. Only a minority of the population have telephones in their homes; for most, making a telephone call means queuing up to use a public callbox. It is a world that, both in photographs and also in the memories of many who grew up at the time, is always seen in shades of grey. We are accustomed to thinking of the 1960s as an explosion of psychedelic colour; Carnaby Street, Twiggy and the Beatles spring to mind. This is not at all how things appeared as the 1950s ended, especially in East London. There, it was a dull, lacklustre world, still blighted by the aftermath of the greatest war that the world had ever seen, which had ended only fifteen years previously.

The decade from 1960 to 1970 was a time of great change throughout the whole country. It is impossible to read any book about post-war Britain without learning that this or that item or event – ranging from washing machines and central heating to foreign holidays – did not become common until the 1960s. Childhood in 1959 was, accordingly, very different from that of 1970. The late 1950s were part of the post-war era, whereas the 1970s were, recognisably, the modern world. Nowhere were the changes during the 1960s taking place more noticeably than in the East End of London; those working-class districts lying between the City of London and the River Lea.

One aspect of change was, of course, the increasing level of affluence, with children expecting more material possessions and wanting regular 'pocket money'. This was no more than a reflection of how society in general was changing. Harold Macmillan, Prime Minister at the beginning of the 1960s, remarked at the time that, 'The luxuries of the rich have become the necessities of the poor.' Of course, those whom Macmillan described as 'the poor' did not all acquire these 'luxuries of the rich' at the same rate. In many ways, the East End was at the back of the queue when it came to the material benefits that were gradually becoming commonplace throughout the '60s.

During the 1960s, this exponential rise in prosperity coincided with the end of a traditional way of life in the East End. The transformation had begun as early as the 1920s, with slum clearance and the movement of many East End residents to Becontree and other parts of West Essex.

It accelerated dramatically after the end of the Second World War, with entire streets being bulldozed to make way for new housing. Large-scale immigration from the New Commonwealth completed this process of change during the 1960s. Over a lot of the area though, as the new decade dawned, communities lived in much the same was as they had done since the Victorian era. A great deal has been written about the loss of stable communities that looked out for each other in the East End, but little is said of the extreme discomfort of waking up in a house so cold that frost had formed on the inside of the windows. There seems to be, in many books about this time and place, hardly any mention of the hardship of outside lavatories, or being compelled to wash all clothes by hand; both common enough experiences for ordinary families living in the East End at the beginning of the '60s. Today, the idea of a small child having to leave the house on a cold winter's night and go into the back garden to use the toilet is almost inconceivable.

Many children grew up in homes without hot water or any source of heating other than an open fire in one room of the house or portable, and hazardous, paraffin stoves. Household items were taken care of and whenever possible repaired rather than being thrown out and replaced. The standard of living for some children was not much better than it would have been for a Victorian child. The best way to illustrate what life was like in that part of London in 1960 is to describe the home of my aunt, who lived on the top floor of a small terraced house in Stratford.

My Aunt Joan and Uncle Eddie, her husband, were both completely illiterate, to the extent that neither of them could write their own names even. Eddie was restricted to the most menial and lowly paid jobs, ranging from an attendant in a public lavatory to a labourer on the roads. They lived with their five children in three rooms – the upper storey of a very dilapidated Victorian house. One of the rooms had a gas cooker and sink. The cooker provided the only source of heating in their home; sometimes, in the winter, all the family moved into this room to sleep, leaving a gas ring on to warm the room. There was an outside lavatory in the back garden and no washing facilities at all apart from the sink. Nor was there any hot water, except that which could be boiled up on the stove. Two panes of glass in the window had been broken and replaced with sheets of cardboard. These made the room draughty and cold for much of the time.

Two of the young children had not been reliably potty trained and my uncle and aunt could not always keep up with all the washing of nappies and so on. Remember that all this had to be done in the one sink. The two small children were, therefore, often naked from the waist down, urinating frequently and defecating occasionally on the furniture and floor. The smell and filth in that one cramped and cold room, where two adults and five children spent almost their entire lives, was truly indescribable.

My uncle and aunt were not an extreme case; many children were living in unbelievably squalid conditions in that part of London in the early 1960s. These were genuine slums, of the kind that one simply does not see today. It is worth bearing in mind when we are waxing regretful about the destruction of old houses and the fragmenting of communities, which took place increasingly during the 1960s, that most families were only too happy to move into homes with inside lavatories, bathrooms, proper heating

and plentiful hot water on tap. They did not bemoan the loss
of their community so much as congratulate themselves
on their good fortune in being granted a vastly improved
standard of living.

Outside the doors of East End houses were the last
vestiges of Victorian street life. Some of the smaller streets
were still cobbled – a type of road more suitable for horses
and carts than for motor cars. From time to time, one still
saw men pushing barrows laden with groceries or milk
through the streets. One old man who sold milk in this way
used to halt his handcart and cry, 'Milk-oh!' a street-cry
dating back centuries. Itinerant knife-sharpeners would set
up a grindstone on the street corner and, of course, there
were the rag-and-bone men with their horses and carts. The
chimney sweep used to arrive at our house on a bicycle.
Chimney sweeps on bicycles; it sounds like something
out of *Mary Poppins*! A photograph taken in one of the
little streets of Bethnal Green or Whitechapel at this time
would have looked little different from one take at the end of
Victoria's reign.

Two pieces of legislation, both passed in 1956, took
a few years to have an effect, but when they did they
altered the face of the East End forever. In 1960 though,
neither had been in force long enough to make any major
difference. The first of these was the 1956 Housing Act.
This gave local authorities a financial incentive, in the form
of enhanced rate support grants, to build taller buildings for
housing council tenants. Anything over six floors attracted
very favourable terms indeed. Up until this time, local
authorities had been erecting sprawling, brick-built blocks
of flats or ordinary houses; most blocks were no more

than three floors. As the '60s drew on, the trend was for estates of tower blocks – fifteen, twenty or even twenty-five storeys high. Now, while those being re-housed from slums were initially delighted to be given a flat on the eighteenth floor of a tower block – with central heating, a bathroom and running hot water – the fact is that such blocks might almost have been specially designed to disrupt the ties which bound the old communities together. We shall see more about this later.

The other law which changed the character of the East End was the Clean Air Act. This would ultimately ban the burning of coal in domestic fires in London. Since at the time that it was passed practically every house in the East End

A passenger train approaching Bethnal Green station. This image was taken a few months before 1960, but the train looks as though it might have steamed straight out of Queen Victoria's reign. This is what the East End of London looked like at that time. It was a million miles from the exciting developments beginning to take place in the boutiques of the King's Road and Carnaby Street. (Photograph courtesy of Ben Brooksbank)

A rag-and-bone man on a cobbled street. (Photograph courtesy of John Lindie)

was heated by open fires, this too had a great impact. For many years, London had been famous for its 'peasouper' fogs and these were almost entirely caused by smoke from domestic coal fires; not for nothing was London known colloquially as 'The Smoke'.

This was the East End into which I grew up; a place with many characteristics of the late Victorian period and little evidence of the technological revolution that soon-to-be Prime Minister Harold Wilson was to talk about in 1963.

2

Playing Out

Bombsites and Building Sites

It is the archetypal image of East End childhood in the years following the end of the Second World War: a gang of children playing on a bombsite. Bombsites were the remains of buildings destroyed during the Blitz, and provided natural playgrounds for children living nearby. The East End was, of course, particularly badly hit during the bombing of London. This was mainly due to the close proximity of the docks; a prime target for the Luftwaffe. Whole streets were flattened and twenty years later, the former sites of houses, shops and factories still awaited redevelopment. In 1960, there were still many such places, although they were being transformed by that time into building sites, which provided other – although less attractive – places to play.

There are two things to consider about bombsites, which were the forerunners of today's adventure playgrounds. The first is that these fields of rubble and debris, surrounded by ruined buildings, were enormous fun. You could start fires, smash things up, set off fireworks, fight, climb, build dens; in fact do anything at all that one wished. Thomas Hobbe's description of the state of man before civilisation, where each man was, 'constrained only by his ferocity, daring and imagination' is pertinent here. This is not at all a bad description of the situation for children playing on an East End bombsite in the early 1960s! The chief attraction was that bombsites were recognised to be the natural territory of children, and adults seldom made any attempt at all to interfere with what went on there. Probably, they were only too glad to see unruly children smashing things up on a derelict piece of wasteland, rather than rampaging through the streets.

The other point to bear in mind when discussing bombsites is that they were very dangerous and, in many

The origin of the East End's bombsites.

ways, thoroughly unsuitable places for children to play. The ground was covered with a thick layer of bricks, stone, mortar and plaster. Mixed in with this was broken glass, pieces of sharp metal and wooden boards with rusty nails protruding from them. It was rare for a session on a bombsite not to end with cuts and grazes, and more serious injuries were not uncommon. These were caused by the nature of the activities undertaken during play – the most popular of which were war games. It must be remembered that in 1960, the Second World War had only been over for fifteen years; it was still very much recent history. Most children had fathers who had fought in the war, and war stories were a staple of comics such as *The Victor*, which was launched in 1961. Rather than 'Cowboys and Indians', children mimicked warfare with games of 'Germans and English'.

Typically, one group would defend a position established in some ruins. The other party would then launch an assault, hoping to dislodge the enemy and over-run their base. These battles could be very violent and bloody; a bit like an urban version of *Lord of the Flies*. The aim was not actually to injure your opponents, but to cause them to fall back through fear. Half-bricks would be lobbed as close as possible to the enemy, stones were thrown, and chunks of plaster chucked against walls, where they exploded in a most satisfying fashion. Catapults could be used, but attempting to actually hit a person was considered unsporting. The same applied to airguns. In the autumn, fireworks could be thrown. The knack of it was to light a banger and then hold on to it until you were sure that it would explode, either in mid-air or actually in the midst of the enemy. Own goals, where the thing exploded in somebody's hand, were not uncommon.

On one occasion, a party to which I belonged found a length of copper pipe and launched rockets horizontally against a fortified position.

It will come as no surprise to the reader to learn that children in urban, working-class districts like the East End were at a vastly increased risk of injury and death than those in more respectable areas. And what were the girls doing while their brothers were re-enacting the Second World War? Generally, they were building dens and playing at house-keeping. Although there was a convention that girls were not to be targeted during battles, there were inevitably occasional incidents of 'collateral damage' and civilian casualties.

Readers might, at this point, be asking themselves what on earth parents were thinking of to let their children run wild in such dangerous environments. There were two main reasons for this apparent carelessness and laxity on the part of our parents: one is that there was little for the kids to do at home. In 1960, a third of homes still had no television, and record players were even rarer. The average family had four or five children, rather than one or two, and many of the flats and houses were cramped. Having children stuck in the house squabbling, with nothing to occupy them, was something of a nightmare for mothers who wished to get on with the housework; far better that they should be working off their excess energy out of doors. Poverty was also a factor. These days, parents often pay for their children to attend various activities. Failing that, they give them £10 or £20 and know that the kids will be in a cinema, leisure centre, or some other indoor environment. Parents in the East End simply did not have money to throw about in this way fifty years ago. Children had to discover their own means to fill up time.

By the mid-'60s, the bombsites had mostly been cleared up and redeveloped. Building sites became a poor replacement as playgrounds; there always seemed to be somebody ready and willing to chase children away from them. For the more adventurous and foolhardy, the areas alongside railway lines provided a similar sense of freedom from adult interference to the bombsites of the past.

The Woolwich Ferry

There is an amusing moment in an episode of *Only Fools and Horses* from 1985, when Uncle Albert asks Rodney if he has ever been on a ship. 'Yes,' replies Rodney, who then pauses before admitting, 'Well, only the Woolwich Ferry.' Many children living in the East End during the 1960s would have said much the same!

A trip on the Woolwich Ferry was something of an adventure in those days. There were several reasons for this: for one thing, it meant crossing the River Thames, which in itself represented a formidable psychological barrier. For the true-born East Ender, South London was 'south of the river' or 'across the water'; it may as well have been another country. Our explorations tended to be exclusively eastwards: Forest Gate, Manor Park, or Ilford if we felt like going a little further. In the other direction, we might go 'up west', but only as far as Soho or Oxford Street. Beyond this was definitely *Terra Incognita*. But south of the river – well we had heard that people lived there, but few knew more of the matter than the streets of Woolwich on the other side of the water.

Getting to the Woolwich Ferry meant a tube or bus to Stratford and then switching to a minor line which ran to North Woolwich. Much of the railways had been electrified by 1960; steam trains had stopped running from Liverpool Street to Southend in 1956, but steam engines were still used on the Stratford to Woolwich line until 1963. Coincidentally, that was the same year that paddle-steamers were withdrawn from service on the ferry. This meant that a trip from Stratford and across the river on the ferry was completely steam powered!

The railway line ran through Silvertown, separated from the street by only a wire-netting fence. This was in contrast to most of the lines running through the East End, which were carried overhead along viaducts. Once we reached North Woolwich railway station, there was a chance to get close to the engine and perhaps chat to the driver.

North Woolwich railway station. (Photograph courtesy of Fin Fahey)

The ferry itself was a paddle-steamer, driven by a steam engine which one could actually watch in operation through a window on the bowels of the ship; a never-ending source of fascination to many boys. It really was like being on a proper ship, and often we would try to stay on board, travelling back and forth across the Thames. Unfortunately, there was a strict rule that all passengers were to disembark after each crossing, and this resulted in many lively games of hide and seek as the staff tried to find us all and turf us off the boat. There was also a foot tunnel under the river and this meant that we could run along under the Thames, racing the ferry and hoping to board it again on the opposite bank.

There were few places, other than the ubiquitous bombsites, in which to play in the East End. If we wanted to see grass and trees, it meant a trip to either Victoria Park – Vicky Park as it was universally known – or, less commonly, to Wanstead Flats. This was, for those whose everyday life consisted of an unending series of grey streets, as close to the Elysian Fields as they were likely to find themselves in this life.

Victoria Park

Victoria Park was the world's first purpose-built park for ordinary people. It had been set up in the nineteenth century, specifically for East Enders. It had the great advantage of being within walking distance for children living in places like Bethnal Green, Shoreditch and Mile End. For those a little further off, it meant only a short bus ride. In addition to all the trees and grass, Vicky Park had a herd of deer in an

Victoria Park.

enclosure, a lake, a huge lido (or open-air swimming pool) and, best of all, a well-equipped playground.

Perhaps for younger readers, those under the age of forty or so, a few words need to be said about the traditional 1960s playground equipment. In 1975, Cynthia Illingworth, a doctor in Sheffield, published a paper which analysed children's injuries from playing in parks and playgrounds. At that time, tens of thousands of accidents in playgrounds were occurring every year and children were routinely breaking arms, fracturing their skulls and even being killed while playing in parks. As Ms Illingworth put it, 'The younger children were at particular risk on equipment such as the wooden rocking-horse or roundabout, when the

speed of operation could be controlled by older children.'
How very true! The temptation to push a roundabout faster
and faster to hear the screams of terror from the smaller
children, who were hanging on for dear life, seems to
have been all too common. It was certainly the case in the
playground at Victoria Park. Of course, as long as the kids
were hanging on, no harm was likely to be done, apart from
some children being sick after finally being allowed off the
roundabout. It was when some six or seven-year-old lost
his grip and went flying off at speed that the trouble could
start. In those days, there was no rubberised safety surface
and so it might mean a small child crashing head first into
concrete at high speed. Some of the injuries received in this
way resembled, according to doctors at the time, the sort
of damage caused to the body during a car crash.

An autumnal Victoria Park.

A point which must also be borne in mind when discussing playing out of doors, whether in parks or bombsites, is that many older siblings were given charge of their younger brothers and sisters when they went out to play. It was very common for some reckless ten or eleven-year-old boy to have a seven-year-old brother in tow, for whose safety and wellbeing he was solely responsible. Not a desirable state of affairs for either party!

We regularly read in newspapers about 'health and safety gone mad', with children being required to wear goggles if they play conkers. To put this in perspective, we must go back fifty years to a time when it was rare for a child to grow to adulthood without having broken an arm, gashed open a leg so badly that it required stitches, or cracked his skull from falling off a climbing frame or wall. In any East End school during the 1960s, it would be quite usual to see a couple of children with their arms in plaster. Today, this is not at all a common sight, chiefly because playgrounds and parks are so much safer.

For the older kids, the swingboat was always the most popular thing to be on. This was, in effect, a large wooden and steel bench, capable of seating perhaps a dozen children; others would be hanging on precariously. This solid object, even without children weighing perhaps a quarter of a ton, was suspended from a massive steel frame and could be swung backwards and forwards. Children would hang on the ends to push it and there was no limit to its movement. When enough energy was being expended, it could be vertical at the end of each swing. Needless to say, there were cases of children who got struck by the swingboat and had their teeth knocked out or arms broken!

Even the more innocuous looking pieces of equipment such as the rocking-horse could be lethal in the wrong hands. The rocking-horse was another wooden bench, ending in a steel model of a horse's head with handles protruding form it. The device was ingeniously fixed below so that it would simulate the rocking of a horse. The problem came, as Cynthia Illingworth so astutely observed, when 'the speed of operation could be controlled by older children'. It was not unknown for some small child to fly forward, right over the horse's head, and land head first on the concrete.

Whenever older people who grew up at this time are waxing nostalgic about the pleasures of their childhood, one can be quite certain that they have airbrushed from history the countless broken bones, fractured skulls and trips to casualty which used regularly to result from visits to Vicky Park.

The lido at Vicky Park was a real treat in the summer. The pool was usually too crowded for any actual swimming, but it was always fun to have an excuse to strip off most of one's clothes and lark about in the sunshine.

Wanstead Flats

Children wanting somewhere a little wilder to play than Victoria Park needed to hop on the No. 25 bus to Manor Park. This took them to the edge of the nearest place that East London offers in the way of countryside. Wanstead Flats is a bleak and windswept plain, ringed by houses and nestled between the suburbs of Leytonstone, Forest Gate and Manor Park. It consists of over 300 acres of sandy heathland; similar in many ways to Hampstead Heath. In fact, a few years ago there was an attempt by the council

Wanstead Flats today.

to rename it Wanstead Heath, but this idea was soundly rejected by all those living in the area. Wanstead Heath, indeed! It has, time out of mind, been known as Wanstead Flats or just 'the Flats'.

Although technically a remaining fragment of Epping Forest, the Flats has few trees. In appearance, it resembles a temperate version of the scrubby, African savanna: parched grass, low shrubs and a few clumps of sad-looking trees. Because this was part of Epping Forest, there were grazing rights associated with the Flats, and one encountered small herds of cattle scattered here and there (always handy if one wished to re-enact *Rawhide*, or some other favourite western which involved rounding up or rustling cattle).

In actuality, there was not a great deal to do on Wanstead Flats; it was just the feeling of freedom, of not being hemmed in by houses and factories, that kept us going there.

There were small lakes to swim in, one of which had an island in the middle. Needless to say, we used to wade over to this, despite the notices specifically forbidding the practice.

During the bitterly cold winter of 1962, the snow began falling at Christmas and remained on the ground until the following Easter; Wanstead Flats was transformed overnight from savanna into arctic tundra. The lakes froze over and the ice made for fantastic slides – and then there was the tobogganing.

When it became clear that the snow and ice were here to stay for the foreseeable future, children began to clamour for their fathers to make them toboggans. My own father knocked up a couple from scrap wood in the course of a weekend. Now, the East End had many excellent features in those days, but hills were not one of them. In fact, the nearest hills were to be found in central London. There was a psychological barrier in the way of heading in that direction, unless one was

Wanstead Flats was transformed into an arctic tundra during the winter of 1962. The author's brother is seen here playing in the snow.

actually going 'up west'. The solution was found on Wanstead Flats. The lakes there were not natural, but a by-product of nineteenth-century gravel extraction. This work had left rings of sandy spoil along the edge of the lakes, somewhat like low slagheaps. These were covered by grass and sloped down to the water's edge. Although only 6 or 10ft high, they proved to be the very thing for East End winter sports. In several places, slopes ended at the ice covering the lakes. This meant that having gained sufficient momentum, your toboggan would then skid for some distance across the lake's icy surface.

The activities on Wanstead Flats that winter were an absolute nightmare from a health and safety perspective, but fortunately there were no serious injuries. There were a few close calls in the spring, when the ice began to melt, but even then it amounted to no more than one or two kids getting a dunking when the ice gave way.

Games

So far, we have looked mainly at the activities of boys, but girls had their own particular games and way of life too. Apart from the old favourites of hopscotch and skipping games, two very popular pastimes were Fivestones and Jacks. Fivestones, also known by other names including Knucklebones, is an incredibly ancient game. It is mentioned as far back as Homer's *Odyssey*. Five small cubes – in the countryside the knucklebones of sheep were used – are placed on the ground and, depending upon the version of the game being played, must either be thrown in the air and caught on the back of the hand, or one thrown up and then another picked up from the ground before catching the one which was initially thrown.

Jacks was another primarily girls' game often played. Jacks are little metal or plastic shapes, with four small spurs at right angles, ending in round knobs. There are two more spurs without rounded ends. The purpose of this shape is to make the things easy to pick up. A small rubber ball is dropped and, before it has rebounded as high as the point from which it was dropped, one of the Jacks must be picked up from the ground where they have been scattered. The next time the ball is dropped, two must be picked up, and so on, until up to ten or fifteen jacks are being used.

Clapping games also seemed to be capable of entrancing girls for hours at a time. Two girls would sit facing each other; complicated patterns were followed and the clapping was performed in time with some nonsense rhyme. For example, the pattern might be that both girls first clapped their own

Jacks, a game played frequently by girls in the 1960s.
(Photograph courtesy of Bovlb)

hands and then turned both hands outwards and clapped them against their friend's hands; then the right hands would clap, then the left, then both together again. The whole thing followed the rhythm of the rhyme being chanted by them both. One clapping rhyme from this time is about a disease which few children today are likely to encounter.

I had the scarlet fever
I had it very bad
They wrapped me in a blanket
And put me in a van
The van was very shaky
It nearly shook me out
And when I got to the hospital
I heard the children shout
Oh Mummy, oh Daddy
Please take me away
I've been here for a year or more
And now they make me scrub the floor
Here comes Doctor Canister
Sliding down the banister
Half way down he splits his pants
And now he's doing the can-can dance

The aim was to clap faster and faster without losing the pattern or forgetting the words.

Boys also had some quieter games which did not involve charging around like lunatics. Unfortunately, boys being boys, their 'quiet' games all too often ended in injury, usually to themselves. Perhaps the silliest game of this sort was known simply as 'the knife game'. Practically all boys carried penknives around with them at this time, and these could be used for something a little similar to the clapping games played by the girls. Well, it was similar in as far as its successful execution relied upon coordination and the ability to remember a sequence of moves accurately. The player placed his hand, with the fingers splayed out, on a table or desk if indoors, or on the grass if outside. He would then stab down with his knife in the spaces between the fingers. In its simplest form, one would simply move as fast as one dared backwards and forwards. Those with stronger nerves could stab according to a sequence, in much the same way that the girls did with their clapping games. In the most basic form of the game, the pattern would be 1-2-3-4-5-6 and then reversing back again; 6-5-4-3-2-1. A variation might be 1-2-1-3-1-4-1-5-1-6, followed by 1-6-1-5-1-4-1-3-1-2-1. The aim was, of course, to avoid cutting one's fingers off! I cannot recall any of these games which did not ultimately end in bloodshed. If no knives were available, then a pair of compasses or dividers could be used instead. Apparently, this game is still played in schools today, although with pencils and marker pens rather than edged weapons. This is probably a good thing!

Another game to be played with knives was splits. There were two ways of playing this. In the first and most dangerous version, two boys would stand facing each other with their feet as far apart as they could put them. One would then throw his knife between the feet of the other. If it stuck in the ground blade-first, then the boy between whose feet it landed would have to move one foot to the knife; if the knife did not stick in the ground, he could remain where he was; then it was his turn. As the space between the feet grew smaller and smaller, it took a great deal of skill to avoid hitting your opponent's feet with the knife. The first person to strike the other boy's foot was the loser. One could also lose by declining to play any further, although this would usually bring jeers from any spectators. For real tough guys, the game could be played barefoot, while a tamer version – more akin to the game Twister than anything else – entailed throwing the knife some distance away from your opponent and seeing if he could stretch his feet to the point where the knife landed; this variation was strictly for cissies.

Playing on the Railway

For some boys, the railway exercised a fatal fascination; quite literally so in some cases. On the outer edge of the East End, right by the River Lea, was Stratford. Stratford had an enormous marshalling yard, where trucks were being shuffled around endlessly, day and night. Although the mainline had been electrified in the 1950s, steam engines were used in the marshalling yard. The atmosphere of this place, the smell of steam engines and perpetual clanking of the trucks was very enticing; for some, it became a type of adventure playground. Needless to say, the risks involved for small boys dodging around in such an environment were enormous. Not least of these risks was that the railway authorities had a policy of detaining trespassing boys and calling the police to deal with them. The fear of this was far greater than any thought of being killed by a train.

It is these old marshalling yards which have now been transformed into the site of the 2012 Olympic Games; the very epitome of modernity in today's East End. One would hardly recognise this area in the past.

The view from Stratford station at the beginning of the 1960s. This is looking towards the area where the Olympic Stadium now stands. (Photograph courtesy of Ben Brooksbank)

The view from Stratford station today, showing the Olympic Stadium.

It was easy enough to get onto the tracks at Stratford; one could just jump down from the platform of the mainline station if nobody was looking. There were also many gaps in the wire-netting fences which surrounded the marshalling yards. The whole aim of being in the goods yard was really just to remain unseen; slipping from cover to cover and seeing how close we could get to people and trains without being seen. Sometimes, if this palled, some of us would find our way to the mainline between Liverpool Street and Southend. There was access to the railway from many other places besides Stratford. Some people lived in houses which backed onto the line, and there were several bridges that were recognised ways up onto the tracks; the ones carrying the line over Grove Road and Burdett Road were among them.

What was the attraction of being on railway lines? For one thing, you could be pretty sure when crouching in shrubbery alongside the railway, that no passer-by would ask what you were up to – something which did happen from time to time on the streets and bombsites. There was also the sheer thrill of being so close to speeding trains. Additionally, it gave us the chance to test out an urban myth. It was widely believed that a penny laid on the rail would be sufficient to derail a train travelling at top speed. I am able to report, after extensive tests with various denominations of metal currency, that there is not a word of truth in this! There was a subsidiary legend that one could squash a coin to the size of a saucer if it was laid carefully on the track; this too proved impossible to confirm. Every coin which we placed on the line simply vanished forever beneath the thundering wheels of the non-stop express. It was here on the main London to Southend line that perhaps the most dangerous game of all was played from time to time. We called it 'Last One Across'.

'Last One Across' was sometimes played in the streets, when a few of us would dash across the road, without any warning, in front of a lorry or bus. This was rather like the later game of 'Chicken'. One aimed to be the last across the road. I never saw anybody actually killed playing 'Last One Across', although it did occasionally happen. The worst that I ever saw was a friend who stumbled and caught his foot beneath the wheel of a No. 25 bus. It ripped off his shoe and laid bare the glistening white muscles of his foot.

With 'Last One Across' on the railway, there would not be much chance of injury; it would be instant death. I think that we were aware of this, which is why the game was so seldom played. The sheer terror of bolting across the tracks as the Southend Express hurtled towards you is like no other fear I have ever experienced. Almost as idiotic as 'Last One Across' on the railway was pinching detonators from the line on dark, foggy nights.

For those who are unfamiliar with them, railway detonators are small, round, flat capsules, a bit bigger than an old half-crown. They have lead straps protruding from the side to secure them to a railway line – the idea being that they will warn the driver of a red light or hazard ahead if it is too foggy to see clearly.

Pinching detonators from the line was about as foolish an act as one could imagine. In the first place, the driver of the train would not receive warning of the hazard ahead, which could cause a disaster; secondly, there was enough explosive in the things to maim or blind anybody too close when it went off. It was not only individual detonators that were stolen from the railway; on one occasion, a gang to which I belonged forced their way into a wooden hut by the side of the line and found a box containing no fewer than forty of the things. This was treasure indeed, and we made off with the entire box-full.

Actually, detonators of this sort are much harder to set off than one might think. They can be thrown, pelted with stones, struck with a hammer and even shot at with air rifles without exploding. This is because they are set off by pressure rather than impact. The only reliable way of getting them to go 'bang' was to sandwich one between two pieces of paving stone and then jump on the top stone. Miraculously, none of us were ever injured by doing this.

The Beginning of the End for Outdoor Play

By the end of the 1960s, there was a definite feeling that leaving children to roam around on waste-ground was not altogether in keeping with the modern world which was emerging. The bombsites had become building sites, from which children were regularly chased away. Playing in the street was not really possible any more, because an awful lot of children now lived in districts which didn't really have streets at all. Instead, they had the landings outside their flats in the tower blocks, the lifts, stairwells and walkways, together with desolate, windy patches of grass at the foot of the towers.

The Adventure Playground Movement had started in Denmark after the war and spread to this country in the 1950s, but it was not until the 1960s that it really took off in East London. From the very beginning, it was plain that these places of organised play did not really meet the needs of tough, East End kids. To see why, it is only necessary to read an academic account of the rationale or philosophy behind adventure playgrounds:

> Whereas the conventional playground operates by inciting kinetic modes of pleasure, the adventure playground engages the child through a qualitatively different kind of gratification. It induces the pleasure of experimenting, making, and destroying. Yet while the conventional playground is designed to function without adult intervention, the adventure playground is predicated on the presence of a play leader who administers the use of tools and materials and guides the behaviour of children to maintain safety and promote cooperation among them. Thus, while advocates claimed that play activity 'must grow from inside and never be directed from outside', this type of playground required professional guidance, since children had to be taught how to play and become autonomous and free.
>
> (*Designing Modern Childhoods: History, Space and the Material Culture of Children; an International Reader*, by Marta Gutman and Ning de Conink-Smith, 2007)

This is a profoundly depressing vision of play, which explains perfectly why nobody I knew as a kid would have been seen dead in an adventure playground! Nothing could have been more 'autonomous and free' than going wild in the ruins of an old house. We certainly didn't want any interfering grown-up guiding our behaviour or teaching us how to play. As Iona and Peter Opie so neatly put it in their 1969 book *Children's Games in Street and Playground*, 'Nothing extinguishes self-organised play more effectively than does action to promote it.'

Bombsites were exciting places: what might one discover scrambling around there? Perhaps some old coins, things which had once been in the cellar of the building which had stood here until 1940 and then been blown to pieces by German bombs. One might come across literally anything; it was a place to stir a child's imagination and sense of adventure. Looking at the image of the old bombsite, I wonder, would I be able to climb the walls which remain, perhaps by hanging onto the buddleia sprouting from the

One of the few remaining bombsites in London. Even as I took this photograph, I had an urge to climb down and investigate the place. What might I discover if I started scrabbling around there?

A modern-day adventure playground in the East End.

brickwork? (A better question would be, what on earth would passers-by have made of the sight of a man in his early '60s scrambling around and climbing walls in a bombsite? It was this consideration which actually prevented me from hopping over the fence.)

The modern adventure playground (shown opposite) was established on what was once a bombsite. It is bright, but sterile. I can assure readers that I felt no temptation whatsoever to climb over the fence and walk along the gaily painted walkways of this playground. The ground is strewn with safe wood chips; no digging for treasure allowed here! This place never opens unless 'play-leaders' are present to supervise children and make sure that they don't get into mischief or hurt themselves. Is it any wonder that the more adventurous type of child shuns such places? The truth is that many children have a need to be able to explore, engage in dangerous activities and also, smash things up. Bombsites suited the purpose perfectly and provided a valuable safety valve. No wonder that adults, by and large, left us to our own devices there. In a neat and orderly urban environment, you don't really want boys charging round like that in the street where you have your house; far better that they discharge their energy and capacity for mischief on a piece of waste-ground.

By 1970, children and young people hanging round the streets had become seen as a problem; something which needed to be dealt with. For generations, children playing in the streets and on deserted patches of land had been regarded by adults, and children alike, as the natural order of things; from the end of the 1960s onwards, they had become juvenile delinquents, gangs or hooligans; a frame of mind which persists to this day among many adults.

3

Family and Home

Housing

The view from trains travelling through the East End these days is bleak and desolate enough. There is little to see for long stretches other than concrete; blocks of flats, factories and warehouses, with drab-looking housing estates squeezed in where there is room. For many people today, this is the only East End that they can imagine. However, here and there are streets which have remained relatively unchanged and give us some idea of how things used to look in this part of London. (*See* Appendix 3 for a short guided tour of a few remaining such streets.)

As a matter of fact, the closest image we have of what the East End was once like is the fictional *Coronation Street* in Manchester. The houses in Bethnal Green and Cambridge Heath were almost identical to those which we see in the popular ITV soap opera; terraced rows of two-up two-downs, with the front doors opening straight onto the pavement; a pub at one end of the street and a little shop at the other; and, of course, everybody knowing everybody else and minding each other's business.

Not everybody lived in houses, though. There were also Victorian, and later London County Council (LCC), tenement blocks; the prototype for the later blocks of flats. The Blitz destroyed many homes in the East End and after the end of the war, there was a massive programme of rebuilding and slum clearance. The problem was, these tenements and streets consisted of more than just bricks and mortar. They were communities. Another similarity between *Coronation Street* and the way things were in the East End until the late 1960s, is the extent to which everybody knew their neighbours by name; indeed it would be fair to say that there were no strangers in the average street. There was a stability and continuity which is today all but unknown.

An old East End pub – the only surviving building in this area not to have been demolished in redevelopment plans.

People tended to stay put for decades at a time. When I left home in my late teens, the neighbours for four or five houses on either side of my parents' house were all known to me by name; they had all been living there since before I was born. The parents of the mother who lived next door to us, lived in the next house along. There had never been any question of day care, babysitting or nursery for our neighbour's children; she just popped them next door with her own mother. This was not at all unusual.

Well over half a century before David Cameron and his advisers came up with the idea of the 'Big Society', it was a reality in East London, providing incalculable benefits to the children who lived there. Imagine a community where nurseries and childminders were unnecessary; a place where social workers were unknown. Of course, fifty years ago nobody thought in terms of 'volunteerism', to use the expression popular with those who advocate such communities today. Every adult simply took it for granted that any child whom they saw was their responsibility. If there was danger, they would move in to protect the child. If a child was being cheeky or committing anti-social acts, any adult would deal with the behaviour. They did so in the knowledge that other adults were similarly looking out for their own children. It is this sense of involvement and responsibility which was lost forever with the break-up of the traditional working-class districts such as the East End. The calling in of social workers or appeals to 'the authorities' was practically unheard of.

This is the well-known view of the old East End and, as far as it goes, it is a perfectly accurate description of how things once were. Families grew up knowing that Nana was only a couple of streets away and that neighbours could always

A pre-war tenement block.

be called upon for help whenever necessary. Children grew up embedded in a community which held their welfare and safekeeping as a top priority.

These communities provided a great sense of security during childhood, and yet they were swept away by the end of the 1960s. However, the intentions behind the post-war redevelopment of the East End were positive. The housing stock in East London was in a deplorable state and many homes lacked such basic amenities as a bathroom or inside lavatory. Hot water could only be obtained in some homes by boiling kettles and saucepans. Heating came from coal fires, which meant that in winter, only one room in the house was usually warm. In homes without bathrooms, one either bathed in front of the living room fire in a tin bath or went down the road to a bath house. There was certainly no such thing as central heating or double glazing. Faced with such dreadful conditions, it seemed sensible to those in power to knock down those homes which had survived the German bombing and start from scratch, building bright, clean, modern houses and flats. Some residents were offered homes in new developments miles away in Essex; Dagenham, Basildon, Harlow New Town and Debden, for example. Those transferred to such remote locations often felt as though they were in exile. True, they had hot water at the turn of a tap and did not have to visit an outside lavatory in the middle of a frosty night, but the readymade support network of family and neighbours had gone. All childcare from now on had to be provided by strangers.

Part of the difficulty about creating readymade communities in this way was that working-class families tended to get lumped together in one convenient spot. This meant that an East End housewife transplanted to Dagenham or Becontree might find that she had nothing at all in common with her neighbours; thus increasing her sense of isolation. What sort of categories or sub-divisions of the working classes am I talking about here? Well, to begin with, although many of those given homes in the new estates on the fringes of London or in Essex came from the East End, others were from the slums around Kings Cross. The sorts of families found in the tenement blocks in that area were of a very different type to the house-proud families from the terraced buildings in Bethnal Green.

Many families in the East End thought of themselves as being respectable and hardworking people; as indeed most of them were. There was a snobbishness towards the more shiftless and slovenly sort of family encountered in these situations, which were popularly supposed to be 'slummy'. To suddenly be thrown together in this way, as was the case for many who moved to Becontree or were allocated places in the new tower blocks, meant that families were often suspicious of each other and would not wish to either offer or accept favours.

How could one tell the respectable from the slum-dwellers? As children, most of us were indoctrinated with various infallible indicators to watch out for. Not cleaning the front step or sweeping the pavement in front of the house regularly was one strong warning sign that the new neighbour was not a respectable one. There were others: coats being chucked over the newel post at the foot of the stairs instead of being hung up properly, and bicycles being kept in the hall, were both damning in my mother's eyes, as was the state of net curtains. As a child, I soon learnt how to spot the lower class type of working-class home!

For those who remained in London, accommodation was increasingly likely to be in tower blocks. The 1956 Housing Act gave local authorities a financial incentive for this practice: the more tenants they could have living above the sixth floor, the greater their rate of support grant. The result was the wholesale demolition of streets of houses that could have easily been upgraded to modern standards, and twenty-storey towers to replace them. People would find themselves sharing a landing with families from anywhere in London or even, in later years, from far-off parts of the world.

I think it fair to say that if the residents of the East End had been consulted at any stage, many would rather have had their homes modernised than seen them demolished. In the long run, this would probably have been no more expensive than knocking them all down and building tower blocks. The few remaining streets of traditional houses are still occupied and no difficulty has been found in installing bathrooms, inside lavatories and central heating. One sometimes reads that it was the Blitz which was primarily responsible for the destruction of the old housing stock of the East End, but this is not really true. Walking round the East End today, it is curious to see that the schools, churches and public houses apparently escaped the destruction wrought by the German bombers. In fact, many districts remained unscathed by the Blitz, only to fall victim to the local authorities after the war. One example will suffice to show how whole neighbourhoods were swept away by over-enthusiastic planners in the 1950s and '60s.

South of Bethnal Green Road, only a stone's throw from Bethnal Green station, is a dusty expanse of grass called Weavers Fields. One might think this a surviving fragment of an old village green, but that presumption would be quite wrong. There is a clue as to the true origin of this open space in that a large Victorian school stands in the middle of it. There is something slightly surreal about this; an old school in the middle of a common, with no houses nearby to it. The explanation is typical of what happened to many existing communities in the East End. Fifteen years after the end of the war, long after any damage caused by the Luftwaffe had

Typical East London tower blocks. (Photograph courtesy of Kafaffle)

A house near Weavers Fields.

been repaired, the local authority decided that this particular corner of the East End needed tidying up a little.

Surrounding what is today Weavers Field School was an entire community of narrow streets, cobbled courtyards and cottages dating back to the eighteenth century. Families grew up here with grandparents living in the next street; it was a community in the real meaning of the word. The council built blocks of flats round this district, moved some of the residents into these, sent others miles away and then knocked down absolutely everything except the school. This was typical of the changes taking place at that time across the whole of the East End of London. By the late 1960s, it was slowly dawning on planners that tower blocks were a pretty bad idea and that in their enthusiasm to provide up-to-date and modern homes, they had irretrievably damaged the existing communities.

Low-rise
housing near
Weavers Fields.

Many of the problems that emerged with these changes
might have been foreseen. It is as though the planners were
hypnotised by their visions of a lovely, clean city of the future
and did not stop to think of the realities of life for those who
were actually stuck up in the sky in these buildings. When a
busy mother with a baby and small child in the house ran out
of something, she could just pop the baby in the pram and
walk to the corner shop. If she wanted to go a little further,
there was usually a neighbour who would look after the kids
for half an hour. These were people well known to the mother;
they had been living in the street for years. In a tower block,
the situation was quite different. For one thing, many lifts
had a habit of breaking down. If one was on the eighteenth
floor with a baby, this meant really that there was no question

of just popping anywhere; even getting downstairs would be a major operation. Instead of neighbours whom one had known for years and trusted, there were three other flats on your landing; some of which might be empty and none of them containing somebody that you knew well enough to trust with your baby while you went to the shop. Mothers were often effectively trapped in their homes.

The move into tower blocks put a stop, in many cases, to the practice of children 'playing out'. When young children were playing on the pavement in a street of terraced houses, there were always at least one or two mothers on their doorsteps who would keep a benevolent eye upon the children playing. These women would spot strangers and warn children if they strayed into the road and so on. It was a haphazard and informal system, but by and large, it worked.

Things changed in the blocks. To begin with, the place to play for younger children was no longer right outside your front door. Beyond the front door now was just a bleak and uninviting concrete landing. True, there were often patches of grass at the foot of the towers, but these were unattractive places. For one thing, something the architects either did not realise or found unimportant was the fact that the towers acted as traps for the wind, funnelling it down to street level. The clusters of concrete towers also cast long shadows at all times of year. This meant that the ground-level spaces on such estates were always windy and cold, even at the height of summer.

In 1968, a twenty-two-storey tower block in Newham, Ronan Point, suffered a partial collapse only two months after it had been completed. Four people were killed and for many, this was a watershed in the entire idea of tower block estates. Certainly, the trend today is for smaller, three or four-storey buildings. One alarming fact which emerged during the collapse of Ronan Point was that, although the block was 200ft high, the longest escape ladders the fire brigade had only stretched half as far.

Ronan Point proved to be a turning point, bringing to light the dissatisfaction of many of the tenants in the tower blocks. In recent years, evidence has emerged to suggest that the reasons for these massive redevelopments were financial, rather than to improve the welfare of tenants. Many of the new buildings were shoddily constructed, with an emphasis on speed in building rather than safety. When Ronan Point was finally demolished in the 1980s, various disturbing things came to light. The original explosion had been caused by slipshod work on connecting gas pipes, but the very construction of the building itself had been botched. Sections which were, according to the plans, to be filled with mortar, were instead stuffed with old newspapers and household rubbish.

Family Structure

The traditional nuclear family – with a father going off to work and providing for his wife and children, while mother stayed at home to look after the house – was almost universal in the East End, at least at the start of the 1960s. So-called 'blended' families, with step-children, were practically unheard of, as was divorce. I do not remember any single-parent families at all during the early 1960s, and the statistics bear out my recollections. In 1961, there were only 32,000 divorces in the UK. By 1993, this had risen to the point where there were 176,000 divorces between couples with children under sixteen. These figures are misleading; there may well have been 32,000 divorces in 1961, but I certainly did not hear of a single one. They must, I suspect, have been more popular with the middle classes or those with money to pay for solicitors. I can truthfully say that I did not know a single couple split up when I was a child; literally every one of the children with whom I was at school lived with both their natural parents, who were invariably married to each other. Nor did I know any single parents. God help the girl who intended to 'live in sin' with her boyfriend, let alone get pregnant by him! And yes, the expression 'living in sin' was still current in those days.

The prevailing features of East End society were stability and convention: stability, because people tended to stay in one place for decades, rather than upgrading to a larger house or moving around the country; and convention, because the lives of families were bound by a complex series of rites and taboos. The aim was to behave just like the neighbours and not draw attention to oneself by flamboyant or individualistic conduct.

What was life like for a child in an East End family at the beginning of the '60s? My chief memory is that of always seeming to be in the way; my mother being permanently busy with household tasks. This goes a good way to explaining why our mothers were so happy to see us disappear for the whole day and why they didn't enquire too much into where we were going and what we were getting up to.

Family Life

The saying that a woman's work is never done might have been invented to describe the life of mothers in

East London fifty years ago. To take one example, hardly anyone owned a washing machine. Everybody carried out the same household activities on the same day of the week. Monday, for instance, was washday. It was a major undertaking to heat up water for the copper, rub the clothes on a washboard, rinse them and then put them through the mangle to squeeze out excess water. With hot water slopping about and the mangle going, one did not really want children in the way, unless they were old enough to help by turning the handle of the mangle.

In the 1950s, the magazine *Housewife* asked its readers to nominate the most useful invention that they could think of to make life easier for the ordinary mother. Some of the suggestions were ideas like electrically-powered prams, but by far and away the most desired household gadget was something to dry clothes. With tumble-dryers being found now in almost every British home, it is hard to imagine just how much time and energy was taken up by dealing with damp clothes in the 1960s, especially in homes like those in the East End, which tended to be small, poor and with a lot of children.

If the weather was sunny and fine, then one could, of course, hang the stuff out on the clothes line. In the winter, or when it was raining, then it was a very different story. In such a case, the washing would have to be draped on clothes horses and dried in front of the fire. Heaven help you if you knocked over a clothes horse; it could mean rinsing a lot of clothes again and using the mangle. Some homes had airers on pulleys, by means of which damp clothes could be hoisted up to the kitchen ceiling, out of the way. Many homes had clothes lines indoors as well as out. At a pinch, you could also hang damp washing from the picture rail.

A mangle in the
back garden.

Old-fashioned
washboards.

The clothes horses were set in front of the coal fire and the steam rose from them, making the atmosphere damp. Yet again, this was one of those occasions when mothers found it far easier to get on if their children were out of the house. This meant, with all the other chores to complete as well, that the time parents had available to interact with their children was minimal.

Tuesday was ironing day; Thursday was for polishing. With no vacuum cleaners, washing machines or refrigerators, everything was a burdensome chore for mothers. Little wonder then that they were glad when us kids vanished for a few hours. One cannot really blame them for not enquiring too closely where we were going and what we were doing; they were just thankful for the opportunity to get on with the housework. It is easy to see also why our mothers used to send the little ones off with us older kids; anything to have the house to themselves and be able to get on.

Why didn't our mothers do as many parents today do and say, 'Blow the housework, I'm just going to play with my kids'? There were two powerful forces at work to discourage such a lackadaisical approach to household chores. In the first place, there was strong pressure from older members of the community to live life as they themselves had always done; Monday was washday and there was an end to it; that was how it was. I remember a young mother moving into our street when I was very young. This could have been no later than 1960 or 1961. She evidently had her own ideas about life, because she used to do her washing at the weekend. Our clothes lines were empty and bare on a Sunday, but this rebel would think nothing of doing the wash on that day and hanging out the washing on Sunday morning.

Now I don't believe that the opposition to our new neighbour's washday heresy was motivated by religious scruples. Hardly any of the adults in the street went to church, so it cannot have been that they were upset at the flagrant breaking of the Sabbath. Nevertheless, it caused something of a scandal. I recall an elderly neighbour visiting my mother and expressing the strongest possible disapproval of the young woman. One phrase sticks in my memory; the old woman pursed her lips and said sternly to my mother, 'It's not right.'

So our mothers were bound by a code of conduct which dictated what they did each day and how. This desire for the approval of the neighbours ensured that not only were doorsteps kept scrupulously clean, but that the cleaning of them should take place at a certain time on a particular day. One would see all the mothers in the street cleaning their doorsteps in unison; it was a communal activity.

To give some idea of the sort of ridiculous task which occupied mothers at that time and prevented them from spending more time with their children, I must describe the ritual of the picture rail. Many older houses had ornamental wooden moulding running around the room, about 7 or 8ft from the ground. The purpose of this picture rail was, as the name suggests, to provide a way of hanging pictures without banging nails in the wall. Now nobody could possibly see onto the top of these rails; they were simply too high. Yet my mother would regularly fill a pail with warm water and a little Flash powder, and climb up on a chair to sponge down the picture rails. In retrospect, this seems little short of madness and yet this level of pride in the home was very much the rule. No wonder our mothers didn't seem to have as much time to play with us as parents do today!

Social disapproval from relatives and neighbours was the main force at play in this respect; the other was the expectation of husbands that when they came home from work in the evenings, the place would be clean and tidy and the children either out of the way or ready for bed. There was a very clear contract in families at that time, particularly traditional working-class families. The man went out to work and paid for everything, while his wife kept house and looked after the children. No husband would expect to come home after a day's work to a dirty, untidy and chaotic house, nor would he expect to be doing any sort of housework or childcare himself when he got home from work.

As any parent today will cheerfully testify, one can have the whole house in order and it will only take the children ten minutes or so to trash the place. This was, of course, the same in the past. The best solution for all was that the children kept out of the way, letting their mother clean and tidy the house, so that it was fine when Dad got home.

One final example will suffice to show just how busy mothers were at that time, literally from the moment they got out of bed. Because, like many East End homes at the time, we were reliant upon coal to heat the house, my mother's first task in the morning was to rake out the ashes from the previous day and then lay and light a fire. This had to be done if we wanted hot water on tap, as we had a coal-fired boiler. A natural consequence of this was that before the rest of the family had even got out of bed, my mother had already been at work, raking out the ashes, laying the fire and preparing breakfast. No wonder she used to get a little irritable and tired.

I cannot leave the subject of fires without mentioning two good things to come from growing up in a house using coal.

The first is that my mother used to make the fire lighters from rolled up newspaper and, when she was in an affable mood, she would make us swords to play with by the same method. If you take a sheet of a large newspaper, you can roll it very tightly until you have a long, thin, rigid tube. Simply bend one end round and knot it in place to make the hilt and, hey presto, you have a good sword. My own children were very impressed half a century later by my ability to conjure a sword in this way.

Another useful skill which I acquired in those days was the ability to light a fire with just a single match. In recent years, it has never ceased to amaze me just how few people seem to be able to light a decent bonfire. I have watched grown men and women pile a load of branches up and then use an entire box of matches in a fruitless attempt to get the thing to catch. Have these people never heard of kindling? Do they know nothing of rolled up lengths of newspaper beneath a few thin twigs? Is it not obvious that one must create room for the fire to 'breathe' if one wants the thing to catch quickly? Apparently not, and were it not for watching my mother light the fire in the living room in the early 1960s, I might never have learnt such things myself.

Life at Home

A classic academic study in the 1950s and '60s examined the lives of those who had moved from Bethnal Green to Dagenham and found that, just as one might expect, those who were living in new estates felt isolated and cut off from all their families, neighbours and friends. The old support networks for mothers and families had grown up over decades; it was not possible to create a community from scratch. This is only one side of the issue though. In fact, many families were only too happy to move into modern homes, regardless of the loss of community. To see why, we must look at the typical way of life in that part of London fifty years ago.

Most homes were heated by either coal, paraffin stoves or a combination of the two. Both paraffin and coal produce unhealthy fumes and, after a short time, coat everything with a greasy, sooty film. This is one of the reasons why regular washing down of paintwork was necessary in those days; another arduous and time-consuming chore. Many homes did not have hot water on tap and having a bath meant heating up water on the stove or range and then filling a tin tub. In the winter this was a nightmare, because if there were a number of children, the water would be dirty, grey and cold by the time the last one was washed. No wonder that we

At the beginning of the 1960s, many old East End homes had ranges of this sort. By 1970, almost all had been removed and replaced with cookers and boilers.

only bathed once a week! We were fortunate enough to have hot water on tap, but because it was supplied by a coal boiler, summer was difficult; it meant that even on a blazing hot, August day it was necessary to build a fire to have hot water.

I must mention another personal experience at this point. Those with gas cookers would sometimes light a couple of rings to warm the room in the winter. A boy with whom I was at primary school went home to a cold, empty house one winter's afternoon, and for some reason his mother was out. He had seen her light the gas cooker to heat the room and so, as far as anybody was later able to ascertain, he had turned on a couple of gas rings. Perhaps he was distracted at this point, because he did not actually light the rings. His mother returned home a few hours later to find the house full of gas and her eleven-year-old son, her only child, lying dead on the kitchen floor. The old coal-gas was notoriously deadly to inhale. Accidents of this sort are one of the things that we seldom hear of when older people are reminiscing about the East End in the good old days.

For children, the worst aspect of being at home was that there was usually absolutely nothing to do. Over a third of homes still had no television and hardly anybody had a record player. We had a plug-in radio; a bakelite one with valves, which dated from before the war. This radio was our only real form of entertainment. There were some board games in the cupboard under the stairs, a box of plasticene, toy cars and model soldiers, a few old books and that was about it. It cannot really surprise anybody that children preferred to play outdoors when they had the opportunity.

I think it fair to say that children today – growing up in their bright, warm houses with electronic entertainment on tap

A bakelite radio,
which were still in
use in the 1960s.
(Photograph
courtesy of Robneild)

from televisions, mobiles, computers, games consoles and
DVD players – can have absolutely no idea just how dull and
dreary a day at home could be in those days. The radio might
be on, tuned invariably to the *Home Service* or *Light Service*
of the BBC. The BBC in those days had a monopoly on radio
broadcasting, and while teenagers with the newfangled
transistor radios might tune into pirate radio stations like
Caroline, our parents stuck to the BBC. Quite apart from
any preference in music, it was actually illegal at that time to
listen to an unlicensed broadcaster. In 1960, half the homes
in East London did not have a television, and even for those
which did, there were only two black and white channels
and no programmes during the day.

   With little to do at home and minimal external entertainment,
we roamed the outside world, creating our own miniature
kingdoms on bombsites and beside railway lines.

4

Holidays and Days Out

The Essex Effect

From the 1920s onwards, attempts were being made to reduce overcrowding in the East End by encouraging residents to move out of London entirely. This process began with the building of a huge new housing estate in Becontree, just past the suburb of Goodmayes. A drift to West Essex thus began, which accelerated greatly after the end of the Second World War, with the building of the so-called New Towns at places like Harlow and Basildon. Another big housing estate was built on the edge of the Essex town of Loughton. The Debden Estate, as it was called, was vast and peopled almost entirely by former East Enders.

A natural consequence of all this was that many of those who remained living in the East End had relatives in various parts of Essex. Of course, in one sense, East Enders already lived in Essex. It must be borne in mind that places like Mile End were once villages in the country of Essex. Perhaps it was this which led to the snobbishness that many have today about the county. When we talk about the Home Counties, we really mean Surrey, Kent, Hertfordshire and so on. People seldom include Essex in the list when they think about the Home Counties. Respectable people live in Surrey and Hertfordshire, but Essex is full of working-class types with ghastly accents. We see this popular view of Essex all the time in the media with television programmes like *Educating Essex* and *The Only Way is Essex*, which reinforce popular stereotypes of Essex dwellers. They tend to portray people from the county as rough and brash, with vulgar tastes in clothes, cars and everything else.

Staying with Relatives

It has been said that foreign holidays became popular for the first time during the 1960s. This may well be true, but for the vast majority of working people, holidays still meant England. A week at the Butlin's holiday camp in somewhere like Skegness, on the Lincolnshire coast, was the most that children could generally expect to look forward to in the

The symbol of Essex at Mile End tube station.

summer holidays; failing that, a caravan at Canvey Island in the Thames Estuary, a stone's throw from the oil refinery. For many of us, even that was a dream beyond grasp; we had to make do with going to stay with relatives.

The relocation from the East End from the 1920s onwards had led to many families having relatives moving to Essex. I, for example, had a Nana in Romford, one uncle in Dagenham and another in Basildon. Several more remote members of the family had moved out to Harlow and Debden. Since these relations missed the East End from time to time and came back to stay for odd weekends, it seemed only reasonable that they should reciprocate once a year and put us up for a week. For many families in the East End, this was their summer holiday; staying with their grandmother in Basildon. Some were fortunate to have relatives actually living near the seaside, as we did. In addition to Nana at Romford, we were also blessed with my father's mother; Nana at Gosport. For the first twelve years of my life, 'going on holiday' meant piling on the train at Waterloo and trekking down to Portsmouth. The Gosport Ferry, indistinguishable incidentally from the Woolwich Ferry back home, then took us across the harbour to Gosport itself.

Relatives actually living at the seaside, as did my Nana at Gosport, were pretty rare. Generally, one would have to make do with one who lived at least within easy striking distance of the shore. Those with grandparents in Basildon were lucky in this respect. The Essex town of Basildon lies roughly halfway between London and the seaside resort of Southend-on-Sea; something of a Mecca for holidaying East Enders. The New Town at Basildon consisted almost entirely of displaced East Enders, upon whom relatives with children would regularly descend for a week in the summer. Basildon may not actually have been at the seaside, but it was, at any rate, a good deal nearer to the sea than Bethnal Green! Staying in Basildon meant that it was easy enough to get a bus to Southend. Those staying in Harlow were not so lucky, although, even there, there was the chance to roam about the countryside all day; in itself this was a rare novelty for the true-born Londoner.

Of course, holidays with grandparents could also work in the opposite direction and not always to the advantage of children. My wife's mother married a Lincolnshire man and they went off to live in his native county. They were no better off financially than those who remained in the East End, and so my wife's childhood holidays consisted of coming to London for a week in the summer and staying with her grandmother in Bow. There's a holiday treat indeed; a week in Bow!

Days Out

Since crossing the Thames was unthinkable, except for a brief trip on the Woolwich Ferry, and Hertfordshire was *terra incognito*, the options for a day out during the holidays really meant travelling east or west. Heading west, or 'going up west' as we called it, did not mean Shepherds Bush or Ealing; rather it entailed a trip to central London. Trafalgar Square was 'up west' as was Oxford Street, Soho, Carnaby Street and so on. Middle-class parents might have escorted their children to these places, but every trip to the West End which I recall making as a child was in the company of other children. I do not remember any adults being involved at all. Before there were automated ticket barriers, it was usually possible to travel to the West End for the cost of a ticket to the next station from Bethnal Green. Once on the train, we took our chances with ticket collectors at the other end. It was, as a rule, possible to race unexpectedly past the barrier; the ticket collector would shout, but not bother to give chase. There were also good chances of getting away with paying no fare on the buses. In those days, with the old route masters, you could jump on a bus as it waited at traffic lights. If the conductor was upstairs and you could make yourself inconspicuous and stare out of the window when he cried, 'Any more fares, please?', you could, with any luck, travel quite a distance. If challenged, you simply told the conductor that you had no money, whereupon he chucked you off at the next stop and you tried again on another bus. It was generally possible to travel around London in this way for practically nothing. Middle-class parents, of course, bought their children 'Red Rovers', which enabled them to travel on an unlimited number of buses for 5*s*; this was like an early form of the Oyster card.

Southend-on-Sea

Southend-on-Sea was, and still is, the archetypal seaside resort, as visualised by an ordinary kid from East London. Indeed, the town itself developed as a resort chiefly because of the building of the railway line from Liverpool Street station on the very edge of the East End. Before this, Southend was little more than a fishing village, rather like nearby Leigh-on-Sea. Right from the beginning, there was an intimate relationship between Southend and the East End. It has absolutely everything which one hopes to find at the seaside: endless opportunities to make yourself sick by eating sugar in various forms – principally candyfloss, ice cream, sticky drinks and sticks of rock, a pier, a beach,

The author (in the middle) with his mother, brother and sister at the seaside near Gosport on a windy day in the 1960s.

amusement arcades and, of course, a funfair. As a born-and-bred London child, I can honestly say that a day at Southend was the best sort of treat one could possibly hope for.

Southend's association with working-class London is an historic one, stretching back many decades; it was not known as 'East End-on-Sea' for nothing. Although East Enders still flock to Southend for daytrips, it is not quite the thrill that it once was. There are several reasons for this. Firstly, in the 1960s, there were no theme parks like Legoland or Alton Towers. Fairground rides were relatively modest affairs, which were, in general, enjoyed only when a travelling funfair came to Wanstead Flats or Victoria Park. Such excitements were, by their very nature, fleeting and unpredictable. One never really knew when a fair was coming and, even when it did, the rides were no larger than what could be carried on lorries and bolted together in an evening. However, Southend had its own permanent, fixed funfair – the Kursaal.

The Kursaal

The Kursaal in Southend was Britain's earliest permanent amusement park, and one of the first in the whole world, being established before the famous Coney Island Park in New York. Grassy areas along the seafront at Southend had been used during the nineteenth century for travelling fairs. In 1893, a couple of enterprising businessmen bought up some of this land and the following year, the Marine Park and Gardens opened. A small section of these gardens was devoted to a miniature railway and a few other rides, but it soon became obvious that it was these that the public wanted, rather than something like municipal gardens. More of the surrounding land was acquired, and in 1901 the Kursaal itself opened. This was a combined circus, ballroom, billiard hall, dining rooms and fairground. The complex was

The Kursaal in Southend-on-Sea. (Photograph courtesy of Oxyman)

entered via an extravagant pavilion topped with an eye-catching silver dome. In the 1960s, I doubt that you would have found anybody in the East End who was not familiar with the Kursaal's catchphrase, 'By the dome, it's known.'

While residents of Southend itself came to the Kursaal, it was primarily intended to attract day-trippers from London, and was outstandingly successful in doing so. The name of the new park came from two German words, together meaning 'cure-hall' or 'spa'. By the 1930s, when the Kursaal was at its peak, it was known as the fairground of the East End.

It is impossible to put into words the excitement of a visit to the Kursaal. Certainly, all the other attractions of Southend – the beach, pier, cockles, whelks, ice cream and rock – paled into insignificance before it. The Kursaal was, without doubt, the climax of a day at Southend. For one thing, there was the sheer size of the place; some 26 acres crammed with rides, amusement arcades, circus acts – everything that a child from the East End could possibly desire. Although we children didn't care much about this aspect of the Kursaal, it also had one of the finest ballrooms in Europe – the place where Vera Lynn had begun her singing career.

The Kursaal engulfed all the senses: the sight of all those exciting rides, the whine of the ghost train, the rattling of the big dipper, and crack of rifle shots at the range (yes, in those days they really used live ammunition). There was also the extraordinary smell of hot sugar from the candyfloss, the tang of cockle and whelk stalls, the oil from the machinery, and that strange smell produced by the electrical connections from the dodgem cars.

And the rides! The Cyclone was a huge, wooden big dipper (or roller-coaster as they are called today). Then there was the water chute, which propelled passengers in little wooden cars from a high tower, down a chute and into a large pool of water, causing an almighty splash for them and any nearby spectators. There was also the oldest, and probably the gentlest, big dipper in the country. This was the Scenic Railway, which had been operating there since 1910 – ideal for small children and nervous mothers.

We thought the Kursaal was immense in size, almost infinite, although it would be dwarfed by any modern theme park. Alton Towers, for example, covers an area of over 800 acres; thirty-two times as large as the Kursaal. Increasingly, wider travel and the trend towards foreign holidays spelt trouble for the Kursaal. By the end of the 1960s, it was clearly in decline and the outdoor rides closed in 1973. The main pavilion lasted a little longer before, in 1986, it also closed. The site has now been built over with a housing estate, although the main building, with its distinctive silver dome, still survives as a bowling alley.

Epping Forest

Years before the Kursaal opened in Southend, Epping Forest was known as 'the East Enders' Playground'. The coming of the railway to Loughton and Chingford in the nineteenth century meant that access to the forest was easy and cheap. Tea rooms were set up for day-trippers and regular funfairs were held on the edge of the forest. Epping Forest became an accepted treat for East End children when, in 1891, the Ragged School Union began arranging parties there for poor children from the East End. These were financed by the Pearson's Fresh Air Fund. After the war, the railway line to

The author (on the left) enjoying a picnic with his family in Epping Forest in 1961.

Loughton, next door to the forest, was converted into part of the Central Line. This meant that one could just hop on the tube at Mile End or Bethnal Green and be transported to within a fifteen-minute walk of Epping Forest. Days out in the forest were not as frequent as trips to Vicky Park or Wanstead Flats, but they still figure strongly in memories of children who grew up at that time.

As I recall, most such expeditions took place on Bank Holidays when my father was off work. We would team up with a few other families and jump on the tube to Loughton. This was an exceedingly cheap way of spending a day out, as we would not be spending a single penny on amusements when we actually arrived in the forest. Running round beneath the trees and climbing them was entertainment enough. We took with us a picnic, including a methylated-spirits stove for making tea; without which, no true East End picnic would have been considered complete.

Mile End tube sign.

My father also took with him a ball of twine. This was so that he could make bows and arrows for us. I have no idea whether this was a particular East End thing; certainly, my father was not the only one who taught his children how to fashion bows and arrows from branches and twigs. We hacked springy branches from trees with our penknives and my father would cut notches in the ends of them. He would then use the twine to make a bowstring. All we needed then was a supply of arrows – easily enough obtained in the forest – and we were happy for the whole afternoon, while my father snoozed after lunch. In later years, my own daughter was always pleased to have a bow and arrow made in this way when we visited Epping Forest, and I have to say that her friends were also amazed and delighted with them.

5

School

Primary School

The experience of school fifty years ago, especially in a rough part of London, had probably not changed much since Victorian times. Many of the primary schools seemed to have survived the Blitz and actually dated from Queen Victoria's reign. Bonner Street School, in Tower Hamlets, and Weavers Field School, in Bethnal Green, are good example of the Queen Anne mansion style of Victorian school buildings to which most children went. There are a number of such schools in the East End today; huge Victorian buildings, often surrounded by modern housing estates. Turning to the matter of attending school in the early 1960s, it was enormously different from what children today encounter.

Parents were not encouraged – indeed they were actually forbidden – from entering the school. Even in the infants' class, mothers had to wait in a kind of shelter or lych-gate for the teacher to collect the children in the morning or bring them out at the end of the day. The school building itself was strictly off limits. Infants' classes were not too bad; it was once you reached primary school that things became a little tougher.

To begin with, the playground was segregated; girls on one side and boys on the other. This practical arrangement was abandoned some time in the middle of the decade, even though it suited both sides very well. The boys would race round frenetically and the girls would sit quietly playing Jacks or Fivestones. The desks in the classrooms were of the sort which one would only expect to see in a museum today. The fold-up seat was an integral part of it and every desk faced the blackboard at the front; no thought to open-plan classrooms and collaborative learning in those days! There were white china inkwells and, even as late as the mid-1960s, the first pen a child would use at school was a dip-pen. Ballpoints were, for some reason, absolutely forbidden and fountain pens were too expensive to entrust to a careless eight-year-old. There was fierce competition in primary school for the role of ink monitor, whose job it was to take a kind of miniature watering can round the class, refilling the ink wells. For many children, their first experience of using a pen involved dipping an ancient, wooden-handled pen in the ink well and writing a word or two at a time. This was certainly the case at some schools in East London until as late as 1965.

The average class size at this time, in this part of London, was over forty; even forty-five was not at all uncommon. Nor were there teaching assistants or anything of that nature. There was one teacher and she managed to control a class of forty or forty-five children without once raising her voice. Parents today, used as they are to the cheerful hubbub of young schoolchildren, would be astounded by the silence

School desks from the 1960s.

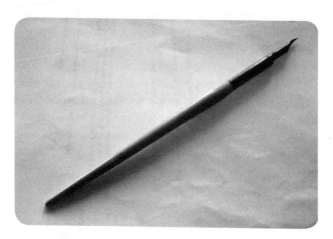

A dip-pen from the 1960s.

that was routine in the primary school classrooms of half a century ago. Bear in mind that these were children from the roughest and poorest homes; many coming from what we would describe today as 'problem families'. It helped, of course, that the threat of physical violence, if seldom employed, loomed constantly in our minds. Children were regularly grabbed, pushed, pinched, shoved and slapped by teachers. In the playground, the slapping of legs was freely used to deal with misbehaviour. More serious problems were dealt with by the slipper or cane. It is hard to believe today, but children as young as seven years old were being caned and struck on the backside with gym shoes throughout the whole of the 1960s. Without the threat of physical punishment, it is hard to see how control in the classroom could have been maintained.

Because these schools had been built in the late nineteenth century, towards the end of Victoria's reign, and had not been updated since then, conditions were often primitive. For example, the lavatories were outside, on the other side of the playground, well away from the main building. If you did get permission to 'be excused', this could mean sprinting through the rain or snow to get to them. Because there were, almost unbelievably, no roofs on many of these toilet blocks, paper was not left in them. Instead, you were obliged to ask the teacher for toilet paper before setting off. This, by the by, was like nothing that we have today; it was scratchy stuff like tracing paper. Indeed, at a pinch, one could actually use this toilet paper for that purpose.

Many of the older primary schools that survived the Blitz were heated by open fires, as at home. These were protected by fireguards, and in the infants were very cosy to sit around during story time. The caretaker would come round during lessons to replenish the fire with fresh coal.

One point which would be very surprising to any child growing up in today's East End, is that at many schools in the early '60s, every single child was white. Certainly, by the end of the decade things had changed, but in 1960 it was quite possible for a child to grow up in East London without encountering anybody but white English children. The only minority that we were aware of, which might conceivably be described as immigrants, were Polish people. These were the children of Polish soldiers and airmen who had fought on the British side during the Second World War and had decided to stay in this country rather than returning to communist Poland. These children had names that we found difficult to pronounce, like Zelinski and Andreskavich, and were invariably Catholic.

I hope that I have not given the impression that life at primary school was one long round of being struck by sadistic teachers and freezing in Victorian classrooms; it was nothing of the sort. Although an ever-present threat, and something to which even the most liberal young teachers would resort to from time to time, the slipper and cane were not in frequent use. It was the fact that they could be used, and sometimes were, which kept us in check. Some of the teachers at schools in the East End at that time were idealistic young women who had deliberately chosen to work in a rough district because they felt that this was where they could do most good. It was a considerable sacrifice, as they tended to live near the school where they worked, which meant well-educated, middle-class women lodging in some of the roughest parts of the country.

Some of these young teachers arranged to take groups of pupils to concerts of classical music and even opera. I remember being taken to see a production of Humperdinck's *Hansel and Gretel* at the Colosseum in the West End. Seeing an opera was wholly different from anything which I had ever experienced or imagined; not at all like the cinema or television, which were the only forms of entertainment which I had known up to that time. We must also bear in mind that these teachers arranged trips of this sort in their own time and begged the theatres for free tickets; my family certainly could not have afforded to pay for a trip to the opera. These expeditions gave me a glimpse of another world, something to which I might one day aspire.

One of the most extraordinary and baffling events of modern life to those of us who went to school in London during the 1950s and '60s, is the way in which the first few flakes of snow signal the closing down of schools. Among both teachers and pupils, there is a name for this; they call it a 'snowday', and the assumption, on all sides, is that it is some sort of entitlement, a bit like a Bank Holiday. Now, while one might understand that schools in remote rural areas could possibly be cut off by snowdrifts during a severe blizzard, it is difficult to comprehend schools in the East End closing down for a day or two, as they do most winters.

I am thinking about the winter of 1962. To begin with, London experienced its last smog, or 'peasouper', in this year. The Clean Air Act had been passed in 1956, but did not come fully into effect until 1963. From that time onwards, there was a complete prohibition on the burning of coal in domestic fires. Instead of the cheap, dirty coal which had been used to heat homes for centuries, everybody would have to switch to expensive smokeless fuels such as anthracite. In the East End though, where central heating was an unaffordable luxury and the coalman a regular visitor in the winter, we were still burning coal at a furious rate, especially when, as in 1962, the autumn was chilly and cold and the winter threatened to be a bitter one.

On 6 December 1962, a thick, choking fog built up in south-east England. The epicentre of this deadly smog was London. For days, visibility in the city was essentially zero. There were no buses; cars sat abandoned in the streets, and it was literally impossible to see across the road. Despite this, the schools opened as usual; it did not occur to anybody that a fog would be enough to close down a school. Later that month, it began snowing at Christmas and the snow then lay on the ground until Easter the following year. Even in London, there were drifts 4 or 5ft high, and entire streets were impassable. The schools did not close for a single day.

At that time, life in primary school was geared towards passing, or not, the all-important 11-plus. This was an examination taken in the last year of primary school, which consisted of a maths paper, an English test and a section of problem solving. The whole thing was essentially designed to test the intelligence and academic aptitude of children. Those who passed could then go on to grammar schools, where they would benefit from a first-class education, at least as good as that available at independent, fee-paying schools. The other seventy-five per cent went to secondary modern schools or technical colleges, where they would receive training for manual jobs, becoming hewers of wood and carriers of water, as the Bible puts it.

Now, even before one took the 11-plus, it was possible to have a pretty good idea as to who would pass and who fail. This is because streaming operated in those days – not only at secondary school, but also at primary schools from the age of seven or eight. By the time you were ten or eleven, you knew whether or not you were one of the bright ones in the A stream or a 'thicko', relegated to the B or C classes.

Even at the time, I had noticed that those chosen to attend grammar school tended to be the better spoken, those from the higher social classes. I wondered vaguely then whether or not this meant that those whose parents had good jobs and owned cars were more clever than the rest of us. Certainly, there was a presumption that children from the poorer parts of London would be less likely to pass the 11-plus and go to a grammar school. In some streets, hardly any children seemed to go to grammar school. It might have been twenty-five per cent nationally, but there was no doubt that living in some places made it far less than a one in four chance of passing the exam.

It is only in recent years that I have become aware of the concern there was at the time that children from working-class districts were disproportionately less likely to get to grammar schools. In 1954, a researcher called Hilde Himmelweit carried out an investigation on this subject, examining two areas in London; the East End and a prosperous suburb. Children's families were assigned social groups, ranging from middle class at the top to lower-working class at the bottom. What was found confirmed everybody's suspicions: the single most important factor in predicting whether or not a child would get a place at a grammar school had nothing to do with intelligence or academic performance; it depended almost entirely upon social class. Put bluntly, the working-class children from the East End had little chance of attending grammar schools, whereas those living in Richmond, whose parents were doctors and bank managers, had an excellent chance. Whatever the reason, most children whom I knew ended up in secondary moderns.

Secondary School

Before we look at life in an East End secondary school, it might be worth examining a few things that were different in the 1960s from the way that young people now regard education. Today, a teenager who doesn't leave school with at least five GCSEs between grades A* and C, is thought to have failed in some way. It is very plainly understood by school pupils that if they do not work hard at secondary school, they may not be able to get a job when they leave school. Every secondary school pupil, even the dullest, is aware of the vital importance attached to passing at least five GCSEs.

This mindset – that failure to work at school might result in unemployment, dates from the 1970s. In 1960, the unemployment rate in Britain was essentially zero. There were plenty of jobs for everybody who wanted them and the only people on the dole were those who were, frankly, too idle to work. Indeed, there were so many jobs that we had to invite people over to this country from India and the Caribbean. One could walk down the street and find a job starting that same day, with no references or any enquiries about qualifications – a sharp contrast indeed to the modern world, where even nursery nurses are increasingly expected to have a degree.

There was also the curious fact that unqualified manual workers could actually find themselves earning more than clerks with five O-Levels. Of course, as the years passed, the clerk could expect to rise to a higher position, whereas the manual worker might not. This was not a particular consideration to most fifteen-year-old boys from the East End. The fact was, they could, with no qualifications at all, earn more at the age of fifteen or sixteen than a boy with a handful of O-Levels starting work in an office. All this fitted very neatly into the world of the secondary modern school. At grammar schools, one learnt Latin and Greek, algebra and economics; the ultimate dream being a place at university. The secondary modern, on the other hand, provided a more practical education, aimed at preparation for the workplace. One would hardly need Latin for a job in the local factory. Indeed, for many jobs, one didn't really need to be able to read English, let alone Latin. My uncle Eddie was of partly Gypsy origin and never even learnt to sign his own name. Literacy was a skill that he had never felt the need to acquire. It was enough that he could sign for his weekly wage packet with a thumbprint or cross.

So what sorts of things were taught at the secondary moderns, in which the great majority of East End children found themselves at the age of eleven? For the boys, basic arithmetic and literacy, combined with practical subjects like woodwork and metal work; for girls, typing and needlework. There was still the fixed idea that education for girls of that class was something of a luxury which they could do without. After all, the trend was for early marriage, typically at the age of around twenty-two. Once she had a husband

and children, most women would be tied to their homes rather than pursuing careers in the workplace.

Something which discouraged many boys from working hard at academic subjects was the knowledge that there were jobs ready and waiting for them, no matter what qualifications they acquired. Those who failed their 11-plus and ended up at secondary moderns did not even take the same exams as those at the grammar schools. In the grammar school, the pupils worked towards the General Certificate of Education; the GCEs, which everybody knew as O-Levels. In secondary moderns, pupils worked to a far less exacting syllabus in order to try and obtain CSEs; Certificates of Secondary Education. Unlike the O-Levels, which, although graded, were really a matter of pass or fail, CSEs were numbered according to how well you did. In theory, a CSE grade 1 was the equivalent of an O-Level, but nobody really believed this. At the other end of the scale was the CSE grade 9, which meant that you were just about capable of walking upright and sitting at a desk!

The school leaving age at this time was fifteen; it was not raised to sixteen until the 1970s, and many young people could not wait to get out of the classroom and start earning. In many cases, children knew already – had known for years – what work they would be doing and it seldom required even a CSE grade 9.

The world of work in the East End of those days was often conducted on the basis of a wink and a nod; it would be an absolute nightmare from the point of view of modern equal opportunities. Fathers introduced their sons to foremen or managers and if the father was a good worker then the boy would often be engaged on the spot. This was especially so with one line of work with a history in that part of London dating back at least 2,000 years; this was loading and unloading ships at the docks.

Work on the docks was all 'casual'; that is to say that men were engaged for a particular job and then laid off until the next one. They were chosen by the foremen on a daily or weekly basis. All these men (there were tens of thousands of them in the 1960s) lived locally. Many of them had been working in the docks all their lives, as had their fathers before them. It was assumed, quite as a matter of course, that their sons would follow them into the docks. It was a very similar arrangement to the mining villages in the Welsh valleys; it was what boys did when they left school – joined their fathers at their job.

It was this atmosphere which discouraged many children in the East End from getting on in life or aiming higher than their fathers had done before them. Even if they did not fancy unloading ships, there was no shortage of similar work available, none of which required anything other than a strong body. Generations had continued in this way in East London; the boys working with their bodies and the girls marrying young and becoming housewives and mothers.

Two things changed during the 1960s and put an end to this traditional outlook on life for children growing up in the East End. One was the abolition of the 11-plus and establishment of comprehensives schools. This meant that instead of being able to coast through secondary school, acquiring nothing more taxing than CSEs in metalwork or domestic science, children from Mile End or Stratford would now be expected to take precisely the same examinations as were being sat in the posh parts of the capital.

The second factor that made the schooldays of children in 1970 very different from those of 1960 was that the world of work was changing dramatically. In 1960, there was no shortage of factories, warehouses and other places into which one could literally walk in the morning and find a job to start the next day; no filling in forms, no references, certainly no CRB checks. If you looked as though you might be able to do the job, well then they would give you a try. You could, in those days, be sacked at a moment's notice, so the employer wasn't really taking much of a chance. People would drift in and out of jobs as soon as they left school. If you had a row with the foreman, then blow it; you could walk out on the spot and find another unskilled job the next morning. Factories often had signs outside listing vacancies.

By 1970, things had changed. The docks were moving away from the East End and manufacturers were also shifting out of the area. And since everybody was taking GCSEs, it became common to ask about educational background. In 1960, a poorly educated fifteen-year-old who was muscular and aggressive could be assured of a job within walking distance of his home. If he had a fist fight with a fellow worker, as certainly happened in the docks and factory yards at that time, nobody batted an eyelid – provided, of course, that such a fight was postponed until tea break or dinner time and did not affect production.

The shift in the economy away from manufacturing and towards the 'service' sector was already starting in the 1960s and it was beginning to have an effect upon how children viewed their schooldays and thought about the acquisition of formal qualifications.

6

Shops

Shopping as a Way of Life

There can be few homes in Britain today which do not have refrigerators and freezers. In 1962, sixty-seven per cent – about two-thirds – of British homes did not have one. This meant that food shopping was a daily event and only small quantities were bought at a time. Milk went off quickly in the summer and there was no point in buying more than an ounce or two of cheese at a time. Homes were not, as is the case today, stockpiled with enough food to withstand a medieval siege; a chance visitor could mean one of us being dispatched to the corner shop to buy an extra loaf or packet of tea. One article that I do remember being sent to fetch, and which in retrospect was perhaps an unwise decision by my mother, was paraffin.

In addition to the coal fire which used to keep one room in the house more or less warm, most homes had one or two paraffin stoves as well. These were horribly dangerous things, supplied from a tank of paraffin beneath it. The casing of these stoves became very hot and was the cause of many minor blisters and burns. Paraffin stoves were also implicated in any number of house fires, particularly where parents had left one in the children's room to take the edge off the night chill in winter. The temptation for children to stick things in the flame, toast bread or otherwise meddle with paraffin heaters was an unfortunate fact of life.

A number of local shops sold paraffin by the pint at that time. There were two types; Esso Pink and Esso Blue and

A 300-year-old shop surviving in the East End.

these were dispensed through taps, like some bizarre pub. What the difference was between the two types of paraffin, I am quite unable to say. I used to be sent to the shop with a large can in order to buy a gallon or so. This was too heavy for me to carry home unaided, and so I was sent with the old pram. Picture a ten-year-old child pushing a battered pushchair through the streets with a gallon of inflammable liquid perched precariously on top, rocking backwards and forwards. I don't think that it is 'health and safety gone mad' to find this a somewhat undesirable arrangement! I was not the only one sent on such errands; it was by no means unusual to see a child pushing an old pram down the streets, loaded with paraffin in this way.

The corner shop played a central role in the life of East End children. Most streets seemed to have a shop on the corner; often counterbalanced by a pub at the other end of the street. It was very much like the setting of *Coronation Street*. These shops sold everything from bacon and cheese to newspapers and string. Nothing was pre-packed and the smallest amounts could be cut to order from the block of cheese or side of ham. There was something intimate about such places and a chat with the neighbours while buying a few potatoes was an important part of the process.

This constant need for shopping was yet another factor that made the task of running a home a full-time job for mothers at that time. I recently walked around a network of streets which survive from this time. They are located between Hackney Road and Bethnal Green Road (*see* Appendix 3). One of the things I noticed, and which accorded well with my memory, is that almost all these streets, at one time, had shops on their corners. These have mostly been converted back into private houses now, but the moulding and cornices in the brickwork reveal their previous purpose.

The tendency today is for shops all to be clustered together in purpose-built rows, but at that time many shops were just tacked onto the end of a row of houses. Indeed, in many cases they had been converted from houses into shops. This is hard to imagine now. The fronts of practically

A surviving fragment of the old East End; Ezra Street.

A typical row of old East End shops which still survive in Columbia Road.

every shop that one sees, from the butcher's to the newsagent, are made of aluminium frames, into which are set vast areas of plate glass. The doors are also made of metal. This was not at all the case a few years ago. Most of the small shops I used to go to had wooden doors, and the windows also had wooden frames, divided up into ordinary panes of glass.

Opening the door of one of these shops would ring a mechanical bell, and so alert the shopkeeper if he happened to be in the back room. One curious characteristic of these places is that they were not self-service, as even the smallest newsagents tend to be today. The goods were all kept piled high on shelves behind a counter; if you wanted a tin of sardines, you would ask the shopkeeper for it and he would reach it down. All this took time, of course, but since shopping in this way was, in a sense, the business of being a housewife, I don't recall anybody ever getting impatient or being in a hurry. This was, in part, also due to the fact that because each shop only catered for the needs of a few streets in a close-knit community, you would almost certainly know the other customers, probably by name. While the people in front were being served, other customers could catch up on gossip.

In addition to the general-purpose shops to be found on the corner of the streets, there were other, smaller places which had simply been set up by enterprising people in a room of their house. The barber's where I had my hair cut as a child was merely somebody's back room, with suitable modifications. The door was their back door and the only indication that this was a commercial premises was the old red, blue and white pole stuck on the side of the house. There was also a little sweetshop, which was really somebody's front room, with an additional door knocked in the wall. I have a suspicion that the rules relating to planning permission, and so on, were not as strictly adhered to in those days!

Before I discuss the larger shops and department stores, it is worth asking ourselves what happened to put an end to this cosy arrangement of little shops scattered through the neighbourhood. The main influencing factor was, of course, supermarkets. Once food was available more cheaply than in the small shops, it became inevitable that shoppers would head for where the bargains were. One of the ways that costs were kept down was by getting shoppers to help themselves and then pay at a checkout. The supermarkets also bought in bulk, because they had storage facilities such as freezers. Once supermarkets became widespread during the 1960s, it was only a matter of time until the smaller shops started to close down.

Of course, not all of the small shops closed down. Corner shops could not compete with the supermarkets on prices, but they could on grounds of convenience. Supermarkets in the 1960s were still closing at five in the evening; those corner shops which survived did so by charging slightly higher prices than the supermarkets and staying open later. People wanting a loaf of bread in the evening would have to go to these shops rather than the supermarkets. Many of the surviving corner shops were owned by Asian shopkeepers, who generally had a culture of working long hours. Native-born East Enders often still insisted on closing religiously at five, to say nothing of continuing to observe the outdated practice of closing early on one afternoon each week.

Larger Shops

If we wanted anything other than the basic necessities, then a walk to one of the main roads was needed. One of the things which I have noticed as an adult is that there no longer seem to be any toy shops at all. In most long parades of shops in East London, at least one or two would have been toy shops. Even if we had no money, we could at least gaze at the windows of such places and dream. I remember looking longingly through the windows at rocking horses and cowboy outfits, toy forts and train sets.

Another type of shop that I remember as a child was the independent, family-owned department stores, which were scattered all over East London. Most of them have disappeared now and the only example I can think of offhand, a little further out from the East End, is Bodgers of Ilford. Boardman's at Stratford was a typical example of this type of shop at the time. One of the attractions, for children, of these big shops was the system which they had for giving change.

In today's age of self-service and checkouts, I suppose that I should explain to younger readers how the larger shops, even chain stores like Woolworths, once worked. Instead of picking up what you wanted and then taking it to a cashier, assistants were standing around and would serve you. Of course, this was pretty wasteful and expensive, because it meant that if there were no customers about – and sometimes, even if there were – the staff would just stand around chatting. In Woolworths, there were counters behind which staff stood ready to serve. Sometimes, they had cash registers near at hand, but in some shops there was a much more exciting system.

There was, until the end of the 1960s, a big store called Sweets at Maryland, just outside Stratford. This had a complicated system of wires running near the ceiling, from the counters to a central cashier. When you paid for something and required change, the shop assistant would place a copy of the receipt, together with the money, into a small metal canister. This would then be propelled, by an elaborate arrangement of springs overhead, along a wire and across the shop to the cashier. He sat in a self-contained cubicle and was responsible for counting out change. Once he had done this, he sent the canister back to the shop assistant, who then unscrewed it and handed you your change. On busy days, the canisters were whizzing above us all the time and most children found them an intriguing sight. The Co-op in East Ham also had a system of this sort.

Some of these department stores became very exciting places at Christmas. We children did not travel far afield, and although we might, if we were lucky, get to go up to the West End to see the lights in Oxford Street, most of us had to be content with what we saw locally. The bigger shops had Christmas displays with grottoes. One had a bran tub at Christmas, where children plunged their hands in to pull out some small toy. Even if our parents were unlikely to be able to afford a new bicycle or electric train set, we could at least see these things on display in the bigger shops and dream about them.

Now, one of the curious things about shops fifty years ago was that they closed promptly at five o'clock, or half past at the latest. This went for the corner shop as well as the biggest department store. There was also 'early closing', which meant that all the shops closed down for one afternoon each week in order to compensate the shop staff for having to work on Saturdays. This had an effect upon the lives of those living in close communities like the East End. If you ran out of tea, sugar or soap powder, you simply went next door and asked to borrow some until the shops opened in the morning. This too was part of the social glue which bound the community together. With no refrigerators, few families kept much food in the house, which meant that most people ran out of things fairly often. The act of borrowing and returning things was itself an opportunity for a chat. Sometimes we kids were sent to ask, 'Mum says, can you lend her a cup of sugar 'til the morning?'

Several developments in the 1960s conspired to put an end to this type of sociable exchange, the main one being that in housing estates you'd be unlikely to pop across the landing of a tower block to borrow a few teabags from somebody you might not even know.

The strict closing times adhered to by shops, combined with pretty rigid enforcement of the Sunday trading laws by local authorities, made evenings and Sundays very grey and gloomy. Today, on the average High Street, quite a few shops are usually open in the evening, but how very different the situation was during the 1960s. Walking around on Sundays, there was quite literally nothing open and nowhere to go, even if one had the money. There was the pub, for which we were too young, and the cinema, which was often showing X-rated films, from which we were technically barred. No wonder so many children found themselves going to church on Sundays and the church youth club in the evening; there was absolutely nothing else to do on that day of the week!

Lack of Money and the 'Never Never'

At this point, the temptation to abandon objectivity and throw my hands up in amazement at the way things are in East London compared to the way they were when I was a boy, is too much to resist! Anybody wandering round the new Westfield shopping centre in Stratford, which replaced the dingy shops that were to be found here in the 1950s and '60s, will be staggered at the amount of money children and teenagers now seem to have. They think nothing of spending £40 on a computer game, and their parents will

The Genesis cinema in Mile End. Built in 1912, it was renamed the ABC in 1960. Nobody ever called it that though – throughout the 1960s it was always known as the Empire. (Photograph courtesy of Silk Tork)

not hesitate to buy them pairs of plimsolls – or trainers as we now call them – costing upwards of £100. Watching children in this area today, it is clear that they are regularly given sufficient money to eat in McDonalds or buy endless bottles of fizzy drinks and crisps; no wonder there is said to be an obesity epidemic!

Even accounting for the effects of inflation, there has been a very real change in the availability of money for children. I am not about to embark upon one of those wearisome tirades in which I recollect that as a young man, I could have an evening out, go to the pictures, get a taxi home and still have change from £1. Obviously, when the average wage was £10 a week, prices were correspondingly lower. However, when we were children in the 1960s, it was not a question of being sent out with less money – we were sent out with no money at all. There simply wasn't enough to spare for our mothers to dish out regular amounts of cash every time we went to the shops or park. I know that for much of my childhood, I had no money at all in my pocket. If I was thirsty, I would drink water from the drinking fountain in the park or street.

This is, incidentally, a minor mystery of the modern world; what happened to all the drinking fountains? At one time, the school playground had drinking fountains and so did every park. Nobody in those days needed to buy a bottle of water; it was freely available. The idea, as a child, of buying a bottle of water would have seemed utterly grotesque. Have the fountains all been removed on health and safety grounds? Is it a conspiracy by the manufacturers of bottled water? How did we manage on tube journeys without bottles of water to sustain us?

You might think that, in those primitive times, the platforms of tube stations would have been strewn with the victims of heatstroke and dehydration, but you would be wrong. Most of us, children and adults, could manage to go for more than ten minutes without a sip of water in those days!

When we went out for the day, it was in the expectation that we would not be spending a single penny. As for drinks, it is true that in the summer we might take a bottle of tap water with us and hope to buy 1*d* worth of sherbet to flavour it with. Odd coppers could sometimes be acquired for this purpose by finding abandoned bottles and taking them to the shop for the deposit. At one time, the price of a bottle of soft drink, or some alcoholic drinks, included a 3*d* deposit, which meant that if you returned the bottle to the shop, you could claim the deposit. Not everybody bothered and so we sometimes used to scavenge around, looking for bottles to return. Four such empty bottles would yield 1*s*.

Homes today, even in the poorest parts of the capital, are stocked with cameras, telephones, televisions, watches, computers, and I don't know what else. Most of these things are bought outright; a situation practically unheard of in the 1960s. If something out of the ordinary was bought for us kids, then the chances are that it was bought on the 'never never' – strictly speaking known as Hire Purchase.

With the casual attitude to belongings that we see today, it is very hard to explain just what a significant thing it was to acquire something like a bike or record player. Some of my friends had bikes, mostly ones which had been passed down from fathers or older brothers. A new bicycle was a major purchase; something which would need careful planning. Hire Purchase meant that one took the goods away at once but paid for them every week for a very long time. Until the final payment had been made, the bicycle, or whatever the item, still belonged to the shop. It was only with the final payment that one actually owned the thing.

Hire Purchase was the usual way of buying any large item: televisions, record players, vacuum cleaners, cameras – anything other than day-to-day necessities were usually on the 'never never'. This meant that if parents wished to give a child an extravagant present for their birthday – a record player for instance – they would be making a huge commitment.

I have seen the careless way that some children today treat their belongings; it seems sometimes that it does not really matter to them if something is broken or lost; their parents will just have to stump up the money for another one. Modern prosperity has bred a generation that doesn't always value all the wonderful things it has. Ten-year-olds on housing estates in Poplar often have televisions, computers, games consoles, DVD players and mobile telephones in their rooms, but these thing are often taken for granted. In the same area fifty years ago, even the sheets on the bed were likely to have been mended. The idea of having one's own radio or record player would have been an unattainable dream for most children. The loss or breakage of some piece of electrical equipment was a very serious matter indeed, because its replacement might prove beyond the financial ability of the family. God help the clumsy child who broke a radio!

7

Health

The Modern Myth

In recent years, a myth has taken root about the health of the nation's children. Put briefly, it is that children today are less healthy than those of fifty years ago. They are fatter, get less exercise and are probably in line to die young of obesity-related disorders such as heart disease and diabetes, not to mention the epidemic of asthma. This is a strange interpretation, as the truth is that the health of children and young people today is incomparably better than that of those a generation or two ago. This is especially so in working-class families, like those in the East End.

Children's Health in the Early 1960s

To begin with, let us at once dispel the idea that children of fifty years ago were likely to be healthier than those today. This is easily done by reminding ourselves that this country's infant mortality rate in 1960 was five times as great as it is today. In other words, five times as many babies under the age of twelve months were dying than is the case today. Let us also recall one or two other facts. In 1961, there were 750,000 cases of measles in this country, resulting in the deaths of over 150 children. Many more were left with permanent brain damage or rendered deaf. Even polio caused eighty deaths that year and left many children crippled. In the cramped homes of the East End, with larger families than average and often inadequate nutrition, the effects of these epidemics were far worse than in more affluent areas. When one child went down with measles or mumps, so too would their brothers and sisters. This led to homes taking on the appearance of makeshift hospital wards, with four, five or even more sick children being cared for. Only those who lived in a working-class home at that time can understand what these epidemics were like.

I mentioned asthma previously, a disorder which we are solemnly assured was of negligible proportions among children fifty years ago. There are two things to consider here. The first is that respiratory illnesses, in general, were far more common among children in British cities half a century ago than is the case now. The main illness was bronchitis though, rather than asthma. This disease, which entails inflamed airways in the lungs resulting in wheezing, coughing and the production of phlegm, was more or less endemic in the East End at that time, among all age groups. We shall see in a moment why this should be. The other point is that there are fashions in diagnoses and treatments. Asthma and allergies happen to be very popular at the moment. Recent research suggests strongly that rather than an epidemic of asthma, what is really happening is that doctors are seeing children with inflamed airways and calling it asthma, whereas fifty years ago they would have been diagnosing those same cases as bronchitis.

Another medical syndrome which was very common in the East End in varying degrees of severity was rickets. This is a deficiency disease in which a lack of vitamin D and calcium prevent a child's bones from hardening properly. It results in deformed limbs and twisted spines.

Medical Problems and the Environment

One of the features of East End life at the beginning of the 1960s – so ubiquitous that one scarcely noticed it – was smoke. Almost everybody seemed to smoke all the time. The doctor's waiting room was filled with smoke and even the doctor would think nothing of smoking during a consultation. There was also, even in those days, a correlation between class and smoking. Manual workers were far more likely to be heavy smokers than those from the professional and managerial classes. It was rare to encounter a young man in the East End at that time who did not smoke; it would almost have been seen as a sign of effeminacy to decline a cigarette or glass of beer.

A consequence of the universal habit of smoking among working-class men, was that every room in the house of the average East End home was regularly filled with tobacco smoke. This in itself predisposed small children towards respiratory problems, but it was not the whole story – not by a long chalk. Homes were also smoky because most of the heating was still provided by coal fires. Throughout the autumn, winter and spring, coal fires would be burning to provide warmth, and in some cases hot water. The fumes from these open fires added to the irritants in the air. Some homes used paraffin heaters and these too gave off unhealthy fumes.

This smoky atmosphere in the home was one reason for the high incidence of bronchitis among children from working-class districts. In better-off homes, there might be gas-fired central heating and less chance of growing up in a smoking household. The situation was not a great deal better in the 'fresh air'. For centuries, London had been famous for its fogs and what we now call smog. The burning of coal in domestic homes meant huge quantities of pollutants discharged straight into the air. In big cities, this was a serious problem. This constant pollution caused periodic catastrophes in London. The great smog of 1952, for instance, killed over 4,000 people, mainly the very young and old. Although this had resulted in the passage of the 1956 Clean Air Act, many poorer people in London could not afford the new smokeless fuel, and continued to burn ordinary coal in their grates well into the 1960s.

There were two practical consequences of burning so much coal, particularly for the children of East End London. The first was that, combined with all the other smoke to which they were exposed at home, many children developed bronchitis. Playing outdoors in the colder months only made this worse, as their lungs were exposed to the particles of sulphur and droplets of sulphuric acid suspended in the air, particularly during foggy weather. The other bad effect of all this dirty smoke upon children's health was rickets.

How could a deficiency disease like rickets be aggravated by atmospheric pollution? The answer to this question is curious and counter-intuitive. Healthy bones need calcium and also vitamin D, which enables the body to absorb the calcium. A lack of either of these substances in childhood can result in rickets. Poor diets that contain insufficient cheese, milk and fresh vegetables can result in not getting enough calcium. Vitamin D can be synthesised in the body by the effect of sunlight on the skin. Here is an interesting fact: there were, on average, thirty-eight hours of sunshine in London during November in the 1950s. Today, the figure is seventy hours; almost double the amount fifty years ago. This is not, as might be assumed, anything to do with climate change or better weather; it is purely and simply because the air is cleaner and there are fewer clouds and fogs caused by pollution. So, even when they were playing outdoors, children in London did not get enough sunshine in winter to enable their bodies to manufacture the right amount of vitamin D.

Perhaps I might, at this point, give a brief personal account of how some of these factors could irrevocably compromise the health of children growing up in the East End at the time of which we are talking. As a baby, I developed chest problems due to the smoky atmosphere into which I was born. These problems were greatly exacerbated by the cold; our home had no heating other than open coal-fires. This meant that in winter, all but one room in the house was literally freezing. On winter mornings, I used to press my fingers against the glass of the bedroom window to melt the ice there. The room was so cold that the condensation from our breath formed a layer of ice on the inside of the windowpanes. I also suffered from rickets, which meant that my bones were, as I was growing, rubbery, rather than hard. This meant that they distorted easily. My breathing difficulties caused my ribs to become misshapen and, in time, my spine also bent into an 'S' shape. The result was that one shoulder grew higher than the other. These were fairly severe outcomes, although far from uncommon. Bow legs, the other classic sign of mild rickets in childhood, were very common.

Cod Liver Oil and Milk

The poor health of children in the East End was proverbial for many decades and a number of initiatives were launched at various times to improve the situation. Rickets, known in Europe as 'The English Disease' and prevalent in this country's cities, was tackled in a number of ways. The most well-known scheme to prevent working-class children from suffering with calcium deficiency was, of course, by giving them free milk at school. Throughout the early 1960s, every child at school was entitled to a third of a pint of milk a day. This began to change in 1968, when Harold Wilson's government decided that secondary school children could do without it.

In the early 1960s, mother and baby clinics issued bottles of cod-liver oil, rich in vitamin D. This too was meant to fight rickets. Unfortunately, although cod-liver oil by itself might well be the richest natural source of vitamin D, it is also sickening to drink neat. Later, it was combined with malt extract, a treacly by-product of the brewing industry, also rich in vitamins and minerals.

With the enormous choice of fruit juices available today, it is strange to think that orange juice was once handed out at clinics in small, glass medicine bottles. Orange juice is, of course, rich in vitamin C – the vitamin essential for the absorption of iron. For many children in the East End, these small, clear bottles of orange juice would be the only fresh fruit juice they would taste in childhood.

Queen Elizabeth Hospital

Children in the East End who had the misfortune of falling seriously ill almost invariably found themselves being admitted to the Queen Elizabeth Hospital on Hackney Road. The catchment area for this hospital included Bethnal Green, Shoreditch, Dalston and Whitechapel.

The Queen Elizabeth had been on the same site on Hackney Road since 1867, having been founded that year by two Quaker sisters. It was a grim, Victorian building which, when I returned to look at recently, reminded me of what I envisage a workhouse to look like. I imagine that it must have been built to the same general design; gloomy, soot-blackened brickwork with small windows; it looks like something from a Dickens novel.

I spent a fortnight in the Queen Elizabeth Hospital in 1961 and it was one of the most miserable times of my life. Not that the staff were cruel or neglectful; they were anything but that. But things were pretty regimented and the emphasis was far more on cleanliness and order than it was on making homesick children feel a bit better. I certainly remember the wards being a sight cleaner and less cluttered than hospital wards are today. There was no doubt at all though who was

The grim exterior of Queen Elizabeth Hospital.

important in those wards; it was the doctors and matrons. They knew what was best for us, and one of the things that wasn't good for their charges was being upset by seeing too much of their parents while they were in hospital.

The Queen Elizabeth Hospital for Children.

In retrospect, one can follow the logic that caused the staff at Queen Elizabeth to restrict visiting. Parents were allowed in for an hour or so once a day. When they left, there were a lot of tears and the children were flustered and upset. It must have seemed to the staff that if only parents didn't come at all, then there would be none of these distressing scenes! As a matter of fact, judging by things that the staff said, it was not all that long ago when parents were not allowed to visit their children at all during the week. Visiting had apparently been limited to weekends and, as a result, the hospital ran a lot more smoothly in those days. This at least was the impression we had. I honestly believed at the time that the staff could, if they wished, re-impose this regime. When I had become particularly distressed one time after my mother had gone, one stern matron told me that if I was going to get upset every time my mother left, she would tell my mother not to come and visit any more. The fear of this threat had a profound effect on me.

Teeth

One thing that everybody who grew up in the East End during the 1960s is likely to have in common is appalling teeth. There were a number of reasons for this; the principle one being that we ate a lot of sugar and very often did not pay attention to cleaning our teeth. Lack of calcium and vitamin D did not help matters either. There were really just two basic procedures when you visited the dentist: fillings and extractions. Dentists did not focus on preventative work at all. I still have a few of my baby teeth that I kept when they fell out, and they are a shocking sight; gaping great holes and silver fillings all over. And these were my first teeth!

In recent years, it has emerged that there was far too much filling of children's teeth going on during the 1960s. It was something of an industry, because preventative children's dentistry was practically unheard of; the money lay in fillings and extractions. The more fillings a dentist did, the more he was paid. A natural consequence of this is that anybody over the age of fifty is likely to have a mouth full of silver fillings and gaps from missing teeth.

One thing that many younger people will find almost unbelievable is that these fillings in children's teeth were, in the main, undertaken without anaesthetic! For major operations, having half a dozen teeth taken out for example, general anaesthetic might be used. This too seems incredible today; that a dentist would feel quite happy to administer gas to a patient and render a child unconscious. This was a risky process that is now completely banned. If a child needed a large filling in a molar, the dentist would simply drill into the tooth without any preparation and fill it. This made visits to the dentist an absolute nightmare, and explains why many older people have a mortal dread of visiting the dentist.

The sheer quantity of fillings was astonishing. It was not uncommon for a dentist to tell a child that she needed ten fillings. Since these would all be undertaken without anaesthetic, it is easy to appreciate the fear that would be generated. Extractions were almost as common as fillings. Fourteen and fifteen-year-olds would have half a dozen teeth out without thinking that anything remarkable had happened.

The introduction of fluoride, both in toothpaste and the water supply, had a dramatic effect on the dental health of children. Most children today, if they clean their teeth regularly, might reasonably expect to reach the age of eighteen without having a single filling. Local anaesthetic is now routinely used for any uncomfortable procedure, and the extraction of teeth is a last resort in children's dentistry, rather than, as it was until 1970, the first response.

8

Poverty

Relative and Absolute Poverty

Every so often one catches sight of a news item in the papers which appears to be so bizarre that, for a moment, you doubt the evidence in front of you. This happened to me recently when I read of a new report, showing that three times as many children in London live in poverty today as was the case in the 1960s. For those of us who remember pots and pans being mended and putting cardboard in our shoes until a new pair could be afforded, this is quite literally unbelievable. Where on earth are all these poor children? The answer is, of course, that our measure of poverty has changed in the last few years. Fifty years ago, the idea of a poor person was judged in absolute terms; somebody who did not have enough food or anywhere to live was poor. There certainly were children in this situation in the London of the early '60s. Today, a family is officially classified as poor if their income is below sixty per cent of the national average. This seems an odd way of defining poverty.

Make Do and Mend

As a child, I had a pair of shoes. I also had a coat. This was the case with most of the children with whom I went to school. If a pair of shoes had a hole in it, my father would mend them. My grandfather had run the last blacksmith's forge in the East End and my own father had grown up being expected to mend anything that was broken or apparently worn out. This applied to everything from garden tools to saucepans and shoes. The East End, in the years following the Second World War, was a place of 'make do and mend'. Nothing was chucked out if it could possibly be mended or put to another use.

Like some other fathers I knew, mine had a cobbler's last; a heavy metal thing like a small anvil. It had three foot-shaped protrusions which shoes and boots could be slipped on if they needed to be nailed. Heels had little metal corners fixed onto them in order to prevent them wearing down too quickly. Shoes would have new soles fixed to them with a foul-smelling adhesive. My father might have been handier than most at this sort of work, growing up with a blacksmith for his own father, but most men in the East End, in those days, would be able to fix almost anything you could think of. They didn't have much choice; nobody could afford to just throw away a pair of shoes as soon as the heel wore down or they sprang a leek.

These days, any East End kitchen, even in the most run-down housing estate, will probably have literally dozens of pots and pans. When I was growing up, we had three saucepans and a frying pan. The saucepans had all been repaired by the use of pot-menders. These were two thin

A cobbler's last, like the one belonging to my father.

discs of metal about the size of halfpennies, with holes drilled through them in the middle. One of these would be placed inside and one outside of a hole in a pan, and then they would be screwed together very tightly; hey Presto, one mended saucepan. There simply was no question of throwing out a saucepan which could be fixed in this way. Buying a new saucepan might mean going without something else that week.

Similarly, old clothes and worn-out sheets were not simply chucked out or given to a charity shop. If there was any wear at all in some item of clothing which my brother had outgrown, it passed down to me as a matter of routine. Clothes or household goods which could no longer be worn or used could often be recycled in other ways. A threadbare old cardigan that could not be darned any more could be unpicked, the wool unwound and then washed to remove the kinks. Sheets which had worn through so that holes were appearing in the middle, could be cut in half and the outside edges sewn together. This meant that the relatively unworn parts would be in the middle and the rough and raggedy bits were on the edge.

9

Comics and Toys

Comics

It was a matter of common observation among educational professionals and researchers during the 1950s and '60s, that children and young people in the East End of London tended not to be bookish. By and large, their reading material was restricted to comics. These were frowned upon at school and it was not unknown for comics to be confiscated and summarily destroyed. The impression that we were given was that such things would harm our developing minds and turn us into illiterate oafs. In view of current concerns about falling literacy rates, and the reluctance of boys in particular to read anything at all, this is ironic. Many schools today actually encourage children to read comic books, or 'graphic novels' as they are sometimes called; anything just to get the kids reading. Even Shakespeare's plays are available now in this format. Imagine that; schools encouraging the pupils to read comics!

Teachers and academics agonised during the post-war years as to why working-class children didn't, in general, take to books. It must have been incredibly frustrating for them in the early 1960s. Here they were giving us access to books written specifically for us and all we wanted to do was read *The Victor* or *Judy*. Why should this have been? One explanation for the state of affairs lies in the nature of the books which we were being offered in libraries and schools; they were not 'relevant' to us or our lives.

I have in front of me a selection of *Janet and John* books, the series with which most children at that time were taught to read. The first book in the series, *Here We Go*, was published in 1949. It was a radically new type of children's book; each page was one attractive, water-colour painting of a pair of children, with only half a dozen large words on each page. Why on earth wouldn't kids in the East End appreciate

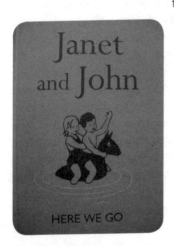

The first book for many children learning to read in the 1960s.

them? The answer is, of course, that they portrayed an utterly alien world to us. Here in Book 1, the boy and girl are exploring what is apparently a sylvan paradise. They climb rocks and then swim happily in a shallow pool, ringed with willows. They have plenty of toys and are very nicely dressed. There is not a street in sight; not even a house; it looks like the Garden of Eden! The world portrayed in the *Janet and John* books looked so peculiar to working-class children in the dingy streets of East London, that it could not really be expected to interest them.

Having graduated from *Janet and John*, children read, or were offered, books by authors such as Enid Blyton and C.S. Lewis. The Enid Blyton books, like *Janet and John*, are about a strange world where children grow up in large detached houses surrounded by extensive gardens. Their families have cooks, gardeners and governesses. It is assumed that the protagonists of such stories are from the upper-middle classes. Here, for example, is a sentence from one of the Enid Blyton books about boarding schools, in this case St Clare's. One of the pupils is a little socially inept and an older girl explains to a classmate why this should be: 'Doris's father used to be our gardener...' There's the sort of statement which I cannot really imagine any of my classmates making to me at my own school in East London!

Even in children's books such as the *Just William* series, this is the same. William's mother neither cooks nor ever goes shopping; she has a servant and cook for that. It was very hard for children growing up in the East End to relate to any of this. Then, in the late 1950s and early '60s, there was something of a revolution in reading matter available for children. It came in the form of comics.

Of course, comics had been around for decades, but often these comics, like the children's books, were directed at a certain class. In the late 1950s and early '60s though, a raft of new titles made their appearance. For girls, there was *Bunty*, which first appeared in 1958, and *Judy*, which hit the shops two years later. Boys' comics included *The Victor*, the first issue of which came out in 1961. The great attraction of these comics to working-class children was that the heroes and heroines of the weekly serials were almost invariably from poor or working-class backgrounds.

Take Alf Tupper, in 'The Tough of the Track' series, who was a prime example from *The Victor*. He was a champion athlete; a twenty-year-old welder who lived in a run-down area and whose diet apparently consisted of nothing but fish and chips washed down with cups of tea. The snobbish athletes from the elite clubs looked down on Alf, but he invariably beat them on the track. Here was a hero with whom we could identify. He used demotic expressions, saying things like, 'Ta, mate!' Sometimes he couldn't afford the rent and had to sleep in the workshop under the railway arches where he worked. This was not the sort of character to be found in any of the books in the school library. He was a thoroughly working-class young man; a manual worker from a rough background.

The boys' comics, like *The Victor* and *Hotspur*, also featured a lot of war stories, many set during the campaigns of the Second World War which we had heard about from our fathers. Again, these stories featured not officers but privates and NCOs. Comics like this were produced for us.

The central characters in stories from *Bunty* and *Judy* always seemed to come from council estates, and were treated in the same way as Alf Tupper by the snooty girls at the stables or boarding school. There was a convention that scholarship girls were always rough diamonds whereas those whose families had money, tended to be spiteful snobs. This was exemplified in *Bunty's* long-running series, 'The Four Marys'. One of these, Mary Simpson, was a working-class scholarship girl at a boarding school. Again, these stories showed working-class children of the kind that seemed to be wholly lacking in the books we were offered.

In 1967, a new girls' comic called *Mandy* went one better than this by setting an entire series in the East End. It became their most popular long-running story. It was about a girl who was dying and, well, I cannot do better than quote verbatim from the introduction which headed each episode of this tear-jerker: 'When Angela Hamilton, a young girl from a wealthy Victorian family, discovered that she had a fatal illness, she decided to devote the rest of her life to rescuing homeless waifs in London's East End.'

In these stories, 'Angel' – as Angela Hamilton became known to the street urchins whom she helped – was living in the East End, albeit from a century or so earlier. Alf Tupper's origins, on the other hand, were never completely clear in *The Victor*; sometimes he seemed to be a Cockney, but at others he came across like a northerner. In both cases though, because they featured working-class Londoners, these comics were read with great enthusiasm in the East End, not just by children, but by teenagers and even those in their early twenties. In quite a few homes, comics like this were the only reading material likely to be seen.

Horror Comics

The British are, as a nation, prone to being gripped by 'moral panics', where some evil is discovered to be corrupting the country's youth and causing an upsurge in crime and immorality. In Victorian times, it was the 'penny dreadfuls' and cheap novels; during the 1930s, the cinema was blamed, and more recently we have had anxieties about the so-called 'video nasties'. Today, of course, it is the internet which apparently poses the greatest threat to our young people's psychological health and wellbeing. During the 1950s and '60s, it was horror comics from America.

Horror comics were rather like the modern-day graphic novels or 'manga' comics. They showed, in strip-cartoon form, tales of murder, crime, vampirism and supernatural events. In the 1950s, they had been blamed for a rise in juvenile delinquency, as it was claimed that teenagers' minds were being perverted by the explicit portrayals of grisly death and torture in these publications. This resulted in the passing of the Children and Young People (Harmful Publications) Act in 1955. It did not really have much effect, because throughout the 1960s black and white comic books of this sort were still freely available in newsagents. They had lurid covers, hinting at unspeakable depravity, and were called enticing names such as *Sinister Tales*, *Creepy Worlds* and *Tales from the Crypt*. Needless to say, they were banned in respectable homes in decent areas, but were tremendously popular in the East End, almost exclusively among boys of secondary school age.

Toys

Many of the toys cherished by children in the early 1960s seem to have vanished without a trace. Toy soldiers, toy cowboys and Indians, guns; one seldom sees such toys these days. Collecting die-cast miniature cars, such as those made by Dinky, Corgi and Matchbox, was once an absolute passion among boys. This craze has also apparently disappeared among modern boys. Like so many changes in childhood in recent years, this one can be pretty certainly attributed to the influence of computers and games consoles.

A clockwork car from the 1960s. This example is from a motor-racing set which was my pride and joy in 1961.

Consider for a moment die-cast toy cars. These were crude things in the early '60s, without even glass in their windows. If a boy was lucky, he might have a few clockwork cars. Two clockwork cars raced round a plastic figure of eight, rather like a clockwork version of Scalextric. Clockwork Scalextric! This sounds so bizarre – something which one might hear about on a comedy show, but I can assure readers that those clockwork cars whizzing round that little track were the glorious highlight of one of my earliest Christmases. These days, of course, boys can not only race cars round photo-realistic streets in 'Grand Theft Auto', they can get out of the cars and machine-gun their rival drivers! There's a trick you can't pull, even with the most expensive Scalextric layout! It has to be said that such games, which are enormously popular with boys, make little metal vehicles seem rather tame. The same, of course, applies to toy soldiers. Manipulating little metal or plastic figures about on the tabletop is one thing,

A die-cast
toy vehicle.

but firing at a television screen in 'Call of Duty' combines the pleasures of both toy soldiers and guns.

Much the same considerations have seen an end to some of the toys that once amused little girls in poorer homes. There was a limit to how much they could play with even the most luxurious doll, but when they had entire families of little dolls, a few inches high, complete with furniture, then the possibilities were endless. Of course, few families in the East End of fifty years ago could afford doll's houses, along with all the figures and furniture, and so the solution was to help children make their own.

Pipe-cleaners and old-fashioned wooden clothes pegs were the raw materials for these. Wire pipe-cleaners could be twisted into matchstick figures, and clothes could be improvised from scraps of tissue or coloured crêpe paper. Peg dolls were made in the same way and furniture fashioned from stiff cardboard. The sisters of a few friends of mine had whole families of little dolls of this sort, which only cost a few pence to make. They would play with them for hours, making them talk and interact with each other. Once more, the use of computers has ended this. Why fool around with pipe cleaners when you can have 'The Sims'?

10

Communication

The Telephone

In a world where instantaneous communication is almost viewed as being an inalienable human right, it is strange to reflect that most homes fifty years ago had no way at all of contacting anybody else. Even as late as the mid-1970s, fewer than half of homes in the UK had telephones. In the early '60s, there were far less than this, and the proportion was a good deal lower in the East End than in the rest of the country. When you made a new friend, one might ask, 'Are you on the phone?' Are you on the phone, indeed! It sounds as dated as asking if somebody has a horse and carriage or whether they have electricity in their home. Everybody today is 'on the phone'.

If one wanted to see a friend or make an arrangement during the 1960s, the most usual way of going about it was simply to walk round to the person's house and knock on the door. This meant many wasted journeys, but one could often track them down elsewhere. Their mother might have told us, 'Jimmy's gone to the park,' or 'He said he was going round Tom's house.' Today, most children and teenagers do not even go to the trouble of knocking on the door; they text each other when they are outside the house. This has removed an entire area of social interaction; the ritual of knocking on the front door and asking, 'Please Mrs Smith, can Jimmy come out to play?'

Tracking down friends in this way occupied a good deal of time, but I don't remember anybody being bothered about it. You might meet somebody else on your travels and so the whole evening would take an unexpected turn – spending time with quite a different group from the people you had been looking for. This gave children's lives in those days a fluid and unpredictable nature, which seems, in retrospect, to have been more exciting than today, when everything is precisely planned by the constant exchange of texts and instant messages.

We were not completely unfamiliar with telephones though; there was always the callbox. In the evening, these would not infrequently have queues outside them. These payphones could also be an occasional source of income for children. To make a call, one needed first to put the money in; 2d or 4d. If the person at the other end answered, then you pressed button A to be connected; if there was no answer, then you hung up and pressed button B to get your money back. Sometimes though, people forgot to do this and so there was 4d, just waiting to be retrieved by the first passer-by to push button B. Many youngsters would pop into every phone box they passed and press button B on the off-chance. This was a bit like playing a fruit machine; it produced a cascade of coins about as often. For the more villainous youth, an old, flat, wooden lolly-stick pushed up the coin chute would sometimes trigger the jackpot and send down all the coins in the box.

It is hard to believe, but even the police were dependent upon call boxes to keep in touch with their colleagues. When *Dr Who* began in 1963, and the famous time machine made its appearance disguised as a police box, this was an effective camouflage. There were hundreds, thousands of those things scattered about London. The Tardis would not have looked out of place on any street corner. In addition to the police telephone, which was accessible only to officers with a key to open the door, there was also a public telephone so that people could contact the local police station directly to report a crime. This was behind a little

1960s state of the art telephones and a camera. Not many East End households could afford these. (Jim Chute)

glass panel. The constable on the beat did not have a radio and so was completely cut off from his colleagues or police station. They did carry one communication device though; a bright, shiny whistle on a chain, which hung in front of their tunics like an old-style watch chain.

Today, the lack of a telephone would mean families losing touch with each other, but due to the nature of the communities in the East End at this time, it didn't happen. This was because most people continued to live in the same house for years on end and their children, when grown, would also usually stay in the same district. Within a half-mile radius there would often live aunts, uncles, grandparents and most close friends. Keeping in touch just meant popping round to people's houses. This was why it was such a dislocating experience when family members moved to one of the New Towns like Harlow in Essex. The only way of keeping in touch was through letters. Of course, the mail was a lot more reliable at that time, with two deliveries each day. The first of these came very early in the morning at half-past seven or eight. Until 1961, deliveries of post even came on Christmas Day itself.

11

Fireworks, Knives and Other Dangers

Fireworks

It is literally beyond belief that throughout the 1960s nobody thought it at all odd that children could buy fireworks freely and misuse them horribly without anybody taking much notice. Until 1976, the sale of fireworks was regulated by the 1875 Explosive Substances Act, which made it an offence to sell fireworks to anybody who was apparently younger than thirteen. In practice, of course, this meant that eleven and twelve-year-olds had no difficulty obtaining as many bangers and rockets as they wished. I say bangers and rockets, because these were really the only sort of fireworks that children bought for their own amusement. It would be a pretty atypical child who bought a roman candle to watch!

It was more or less taken as given that children could fool around in the streets and bombsites with fireworks; at any rate, I don't remember any adult ever interfering. Fireworks were thrown, dropped into milk bottles, cut open in order to fill a larger container with gunpowder to make a bigger bang;

there was no end to the fun to be had with them. Occasionally of course, somebody would take things too far. Jumping jacks or bangers would be lit and then dropped through somebody's letterbox, or a rocket set off indoors – little wonder then that the tally of serious injuries was high. In 1968, there were over 2,200 hospital visits for burns and other injuries caused by fireworks. Some of these ended with children losing an eye or a couple of fingers, and it was not unknown for deaths to occur. Some of the games played were completely foolish: for instance, two boys would light bangers simultaneously and then see who could hold onto the thing for longest. This game alone was responsible for many injuries.

Since 1997, some kinds of fireworks have been made illegal in this country; these include all the really enjoyable ones! Fancy passing a law to ban bangers! Even the relatively innocuous jumping jack is now outlawed. For younger readers, the jumping jack was a bunched up tube of gunpowder which would explode erratically and at intervals, jumping up in the air each time. Needless to say, this caused stampedes of nervous children, at least one of whom was bound to stumble and almost fall into the bonfire.

Knives

During the 1960s, I doubt that there was a single boy in the East End over the age of seven or eight who did not habitually carry a knife. These were mostly penknives, otherwise known as pocket knives; the type where the blade folds into the handle. I do not recall, nor have I ever heard of, anybody ever using one of these knives to stab anybody at this time; they were simply what boys had in their pockets. It was an expected thing in those days that boys had knives with them. They could be used not just to cut string or carve wood – the grander ones also had can-openers and, of course, the gadget to remove stones from horses' hooves. I have never, in the entire course of my life, ever heard of anybody having to deal with a horse getting a stone trapped in its hoof, but there it is; had such an accident occurred, there would have been no shortage of boys in East London equipped to tackle the job.

The penknife was a favourite souvenir to purchase on school trips or days out. Even cathedrals sold penknives, with pictures of the town on their cases. The idea that a child would use the thing to harm another child with was literally unheard of. The carrying of knives was not limited to penknives either. Scouts often carried large-sheath knives on their belts without anyone batting an eyelid. I remember a teacher once trying to fix a screw on his desk and asking if any of us had a penknife. When he drew a blank, he chided us gently for being a pretty poor bunch compared to the boys with whom he had gone to school. He seemed to take it as a matter of course that any boy worth his salt would be sure to have a knife with him at all times. Imagine a teacher today encouraging his pupils to carry knives! It would be front-page news.

This is not say, of course, that nobody ever got stabbed in the East End of fifty years ago. It certainly happened that Teddy Boys in the late 1950s, and Mods and Rockers in the 1960s, occasionally went for each other with knives, but these were isolated incidents. The death-toll did not run into hundreds annually as it does today. Perhaps the fact that, until 1964, anybody knifing somebody to death in this way faced the prospect of being hanged for their crime, acted to discourage such behaviour.

The only person, in general, who was liable to be harmed by a boy's knife, was the boy himself, and such injuries were only minor. It is truly extraordinary to read in the newspapers today of attempts to make the carrying of any knife by a young person into a serious criminal offence, punishable by a mandatory custodial sentence. If such a law had been enacted fifty years ago, it would have meant the imprisonment of practically every boy in East London!

Stranger Danger

Without doubt, the single greatest fear of all parents in this country is that their children might be abducted by some roaming homicidal maniac. It is this anxiety, above all others, which accounts for the reluctance of so many parents to allow their children greater freedom of movement. It is the reason why so few parents let their children walk to school or play in parks without strict adult supervision. Only forty years ago, eighty per cent of seven and eight-year-olds walked alone to school; today, a child of seven walking alone to school would be regarded as being in mortal danger. There have actually been cases in the last year or so of schools threatening to inform social services when they have spotted eight or nine-year-old children arriving at school unescorted by an adult.

This fear of one's child being taken by a stranger was all but unknown fifty years ago. The fact is that the murder of children by somebody completely unknown to them is, and always has been, very rare. Perhaps ten children a year are killed in this way and this figure has remained unchanged since the end of the Second World War, almost seventy years ago. Although it looms in the minds of both parents and children, the risk from 'stranger danger' is negligible.

The casual minor abuse of children by those known to them has always been vastly more common than their abduction, rape or murder by strangers. There is regular outrage at the supposedly ridiculous regulations now surrounding those who work with children, either in a paid or voluntary capacity. This is 'health and safety gone mad'; old Granny Jones has worked with the choir for over fifty years! What possible reason could there be for requiring her to have a CRB check?

In a modern society, which takes the sexual abuse of children very seriously, it might be hard to imagine what the situation was once like in London, particularly in working-class areas. It seems that, in Britain, there has been an erosion in the respect children show to authority figures such as police, teachers, parents and adults in general over the last few decades. In some ways, this has been negative; in others, it has been a positive blessing. One of the things that some children in the 1960s, growing up in the working-class districts of East London, were well aware of was that some of those in authority, with whom they came into regular contact, had an unhealthy interest in them. These might be teachers, vicars, scoutmasters and youth-club workers.

The problem was that they were usually 'educated', and our parents almost invariably accepted their word against ours. If your teacher said you had been misbehaving, then that was what you had been doing. As a child, one knew that two factors were at work here, although we would, of course, have been wholly unable to articulate them. In the first place, there was a general conspiracy of adults. They all stuck together and stood up for each other, ignoring the complaints of children. Secondly, people like teachers and vicars – those who spoke 'properly' – would be given a good deal more credence by our working-class parents than we were ourselves. If our version of events was contradicted by the teacher or vicar, then the educated adult's version would be taken as the definitive one.

Now, speaking in general, this was very right and proper. Obviously, we kids used to try and lie our way out of trouble and parents were wise to take the teachers story as more accurate than ours. If the teacher said that we were too prone to mucking about in class and distracting others who wished to work, then we would naturally deny this vehemently. Faced with these two diametrically opposed and conflicting accounts, our parents almost invariably took the teacher's story as being true. The problem arose when adults in authority had potential to be inappropriate with children – I am thinking here of teachers who invited children round to their homes, others who gave private tuition to pupils after school, vicars running confirmation classes, and scoutmasters who went camping with their boys. We children all knew which adults to avoid, but I don't believe any of us ever mentioned such things except to other children. I knew classmates who were given 10s for visiting one particular teacher, and others who always had plenty of sweets after their music lessons. One scoutmaster was famous for engaging in play fights at camp with boys in their pyjamas.

Sexual abuse of children was rife in the East End at that time, partly because of the power imbalance between working-class children and middle-class, professional adults. A child from a poor home in Stepney would also be more impressed with a bag of sweets or gift of half a crown than would a kid from Hampstead. He might be more likely to keep his mouth shut afterwards as well.

There was another reason why nobody 'told'. The whole topic of sex in those days was shrouded with shame and embarrassment. One simply did not talk about it to, or in front of, adults; it was 'dirty'. The very idea of broaching a subject with one's parents which would entail talking about sex was simply unthinkable. I doubt if our parents would have thanked us anyway.

The Sex Life of Teenagers

This will probably be the shortest section in the whole book, because adolescents up to the age of eighteen or so had very little opportunity to engage in full sexual relations. There were several reasons for this. There was a very strict moral code in force in the 1960s, which frowned upon pre-marital relations and regarded illegitimate babies as little short of a disaster. Parents, although reluctant to discuss the matter openly, knew perfectly well what their sons and daughters might get up to given half a chance, and made damned sure that they didn't get even that half chance. It was tacitly assumed that friendships between boys and girl might end up in a sexually compromising situation if active steps were not taken to prevent it. What sort of steps? Well, strict curfews for girls were one way, with eighteen-year-olds often being expected to be home by half-past ten. Bedrooms were off-limits. I courted a girl for eighteen months and, despite being a frequent visitor at her house, never once saw the inside of her bedroom. Most parents enforced such rules and if a boy did visit a girl's room, the invariable rule was that the door must remain open. Simple rules of this sort severely limited the sex lives of adolescents and, as a result, teenage pregnancy was all but unheard of.

In the East End, traditional sexual morality was the rule, with girls not expecting to 'go all the way' until their wedding night, or at the very least until they were officially engaged. Fathers were zealous in guarding their daughters and the shotgun wedding was still a regular event. Unmarried girls had a terror of 'getting into trouble' – the commonest euphemism for unplanned pregnancy.

Something else worked to discourage early sexual activity as well. These days, the defining lines between childhood and adulthood are far more blurred than they once were. Children as young as seven can be seen wearing makeup and padded bras, and a child of fourteen is often indistinguishable from a young adult of eighteen or nineteen. Fifty years ago, childhood was prolonged a little, which meant that the age at which sexual activity began was delayed by a few years. This made all the difference; a girl of nineteen is far more able to handle a sexual relationship than one of thirteen or fourteen.

The distinction between young girls and adult women was marked with stages, such as the age at which a girl began using makeup or wearing jewellery, tights and high heels. This meant that young girls tended to look as such, rather than appearing like grown women. This had an effect on how they were perceived and treated, which, in turn, acted to delay the onset of sexual activity. Today, the median age for a girl to first engage in sexual activity is fourteen. It would have been rare for a fourteen-year-old girl to 'go all the way' fifty years ago.

12

Religion

A Common Background

Something which those under the age of fifty or so might find hard to grasp is the extent to which, in the 1960s, our lives were underpinned and permeated by religion. This is not to say that those with whom I grew up were particularly pious; my family certainly were not. It is a curious thing, but in this country church attendance and religious observance has always been linked to class and income. Even at the height of the Victorian era, when we have the impression that everybody flocked to church on Sundays, the truth is that the working classes were the despair of the clergy! This trend for working-class people to avoid church was still pretty strong when I was growing up. I would definitely have been seen as a little odd had I been attending church voluntarily. In what sense do I mean it then when I say that the lives of children in the East End of fifty years ago were underpinned by religion?

We might have been an irreligious bunch in our neighbourhood, but many, perhaps most of us, found

ourselves in church at least once a month. There were a
number of reasons for this. Although few parents attended
church themselves, or even believed in God, quite a number
felt that it was good for children to go to Sunday School. I
hope that I am not being unduly cynical when I suggest that
a lot of the time this was so that Mum could get on with
cooking the lunch and Dad could settle down with the *News
of the World*. Still, for whatever reason, an awful lot of
children in the East End went to Sunday School when they
were little. There were perks to this; not the least of these
being outings and treats from time to time.

Older children and teenagers also went to church
quite a lot, because they belonged to either uniformed
organisations, such as the Boys' Brigade and Girl Guides,
or went to a church youth club. Membership of such things
was a good deal more common fifty years ago than it is
today, because there was often precious little else to do
in the evenings. In most cases, church attendance was a
condition of membership. The Boys' Brigade in particular
was very popular with teenagers. The local group had a band
and they used to march through the streets on Sundays,
playing on their way to church. It has been many years since
I have seen anything of this sort.

Religion in those days meant Christianity, or more
specifically the Church of England. We knew from our
earliest years that the space marked 'religion' on forms
meant putting down 'C of E'. Of course, there were those
who wrote 'RC'. These were chiefly Irish or Polish and their
religion was viewed as being slightly alien, although we
knew little enough of any supposed doctrinal differences
that separated us from Catholics; it was just that they were

different – 'normal' people were C of E. Then, of course, there were Jewish people. Already, by that time, the Jewish community were moving away from Whitechapel and Stepney, and heading to more respectable districts such as Stamford Hill or Ilford. In our school, when they were excused from religious observance at assembly, the headmaster referred to them as 'the Hebrews'.

It was taken more or less as a given at school, right from the beginning, that we were all Christians. In the infants' class, the day began with prayers and by primary school we were singing hymns at the start of each day. By the time we reached secondary school, assembly had assumed the nature of a proper church service, with hymns, prayers and readings from books about missionaries like Gladys Aylward. We took all this for granted; it was part of what I described earlier when I wrote of religion being a foundation to life at this time. We did not have a lesson called Religious Studies, as children today have; instead we had 'Scripture', which concerned itself entirely with the teachings of the Bible. I would say that every child at school could recite the Lord's Prayer and had more than a nodding acquaintance with the Ten Commandments. I must emphasise that I did not attend a Church school, or 'faith' school as we are now supposed to call them. This was just an ordinary state secondary school.

Some of the disputes that we had as kids would have delighted a medieval theologian. For example, there was the vexed issue of whether one should pronounce the word 'amen', at the end of the Lord's Prayer, as ah-men or a-men. There was quite fierce debate about this, with the class being divided roughly in half. Then there was the correct pronunciation of the word 'aye'; as in the line from the hymn, 'For his mercies aye endure'. Never mind that none of us had the faintest idea what the word meant in this context; our only interest in the matter was whether to pronounce it as 'eye' or 'a'.

That we had some sort of vague feelings about the sanctity of religion is indicated by our most solemn oath and assurance that we were telling the unvarnished truth, which was 'God's honour'. This vow was absolutely binding and was not negated by any of the usual artifices such as crossing fingers while speaking it. If you said 'God's honour', then your hearers knew that you spoke truly. Nobody would dream of swearing falsely in such a way. There is something magnificently archaic about such a solemn oath.

I am sure that it was not done intentionally by those running the churches, but our very poverty helped draw us into religious observance. I have explained that many children from the area were from families who could not afford a proper holiday. For these children, the annual camp for Girl Guides, Boy's Brigade or other church-related organisations meant a week at the seaside or in the country. The leaders of these uniformed groups were, at that time, quite strict about members attending church parades, which were held at least once a month and often more frequently. Membership of youth clubs was often similarly contingent upon church attendance. Combine this with the number of kids who were packed off to Sunday School, and a picture emerges of young people growing up with a pretty sound grounding in the Christian faith – even though, in most cases, their parents had no religious beliefs at all.

13

Immigration

The Way Things Were

It is a myth that London has always been a multicultural city, as has been suggested with eighteenth-century portraits showing black page boys, mentions of freed slaves who settled here, and broad hints that even before large-scale immigration began in the 1950s from the so-called New Commonwealth, that there were plenty of black and Asian people living in the city.

For anybody who actually grew up in East London during the 1950s and '60s, these assertions are absurd. I grew up and attended a number of schools in East London and did not even speak to a black person until after I had left school. This was not because I was a racist bigot; it is simply that there was not a single black person or Asian in any of my classes at school.

Now this is not to say that the East End has not, over the centuries, attracted immigrants and asylum seekers. It certainly has, and their influence may still be seen there. In the eighteenth century, French Protestants, the Huguenots, settled in Whitechapel and began the association of that district with the rag trade. A century later, Jewish people from Eastern Europe and Russia displaced the French but continued their tradition of clothes making. Chinese settlers came to Limehouse, and after the Second World War there were quite a few Polish people in my part of London. There were also a few Lascars, sailors of Indian origin, living down by the docks. These earlier arrivals came gradually though.

Of course, as children growing up in that part of London, we were vaguely aware that some of our schoolmates were not of the same, traditional, Church of England origin as ourselves, but the differences were minor. They might have had exotic names, and perhaps they followed a different line in religion – being Roman Catholics or attending a synagogue instead of a church – but apart from these trifling differences, there was no great divide. They had grown up in the same district and spoke the same language; we shared a common heritage with them in many ways. At the very least, they were Europeans and we had much in common with them.

In those days, we took this shared racial and common cultural background for granted. One talked of 'flesh colour', meaning a pale peachy shade, without any thought for how we might be excluding those with higher levels of melanin in their skin than us. (I shall say nothing of the soft-furnishings section of a Stratford department store, which, shockingly, had curtains advertised as being 'Nigger Brown' when I was little.) I have in front of me a favourite childhood book; *The Big Wonder Book of the World*. Its aim was to introduce children to geography in a simple fashion. The first double spread is a map of the world with colourful pictures to illustrate various countries. America has scientists in white coats and Italy has a Renaissance cathedral. There are two pictures illustrating Africa: one is of a half-naked woman carrying a jar of water balanced on her head; the other is a village of mud huts with a man standing in the foreground, clutching a bunch of spears.

Subconsciously, before they had ever met a black person in real life, the children with whom I was at school were conditioned to see them as outsiders. White European was our default setting; anything else set alarm bells ringing. Something which must be borne in mind is that the East End was a very conservative place. New things and new ideas were not always welcomed unreservedly. If Nana and Mum had cleaned the front step and boiled the net curtains each week, then you were expected to do the same. Rebels, mavericks and outsiders were eyed a little askance.

The Arrival of Immigrants from the New Commonwealth

The first areas of London to become the focus of black settlement were Brixton and Notting Hill. Called at the time 'coloured people', these communities did not start moving into the East End until the 1960s. When they did, they encountered hostility. As a child, I was perfectly aware of what was being said and done about the perceived 'problem' of immigrants moving into the area. Until the mid-1960s, there was nothing at all to stop pubs from refusing to serve black people, and I clearly remember signs offering a room to rent which read, 'Sorry, no coloureds'. The letters 'KBW' would commonly be seen painted on walls: this stands for 'Keep Britain White'. I knew that many adults were bitterly opposed to the idea of ethnic minorities living next door to them, or even in the same street.

To be fair to the East Enders, some of this reluctance to welcome outsiders would have been exactly the same if it was people from other parts of Britain who were coming in from other places. It was not so much about race or xenophobia, as a desire to maintain the same composition of the close-knit local communities, and not see them disrupted by an influx of 'outsiders'. Unfortunately, as we have seen, those communities were already being broken up, and although some blamed 'coloured' immigration for this, the fact is it merely contributed to a process which was already well under way. I honestly believe that there would have been just as much resentment if those coming in from outside had been white, English people from Liverpool, say. The defining feature was not race or ethnicity, but that these people came from outside the East End; and there seemed, from the point of view of many, to be an awful lot of them.

Certainly, as a child, I encountered what the Museum of London refers to in a display as the 'casual racism' of the time. Even this, though, is not as simple as it might at first appear to somebody unfamiliar with this part of London. East Enders had various more or less unflattering expressions to denote practically everybody and everything. Colloquial expressions and their rhyming slang equivalents were used freely; they were not as much a statement of political belief or ingrained prejudice as they are today.

A man might perhaps remark of a workmate who declined to do a shift on Saturdays, 'Oh, Izzy's a four by two [Jew].' Or a man could mention that a bunch of razor blades had moved into the next street (razor blades – spades). Now some conversation of this sort might very well upset modern sensibilities, but it did not in any way indicate hostile feeling towards those to whom it was directed. It was just that East Enders had a ready stock of insulting expressions about everybody! A churchgoer might be referred to behind his back as a 'Holy Joe'; anybody at all out of the ordinary could be sure to be the object of remark.

Still, having said all this, it must be admitted that immigrants from India, Pakistan and the West Indies were not welcomed with open arms when they began to move into the East End in the 1960s. They were allocated council houses and, of course, every council house which went to a family from Jamaica or Pakistan meant one less for a member of a family which might have been living in the East End for a century or so. It did create ill feeling. Things might have been easier if the transition had been managed a little more tactfully and with some planning. Nobody really objected to Polish families living next door, partly because they were white Europeans, but also because they remained very definitely a minority wherever they settled. The same was true of other groups who found refuge in the East End over the years; there were a limited number of them and, by and large, they had similar habits to us and tried to fit in. This was not so much the case with black and Asian immigrants.

Naturally, new immigrants tended to bring with them their own ways of doing things – unfamiliar customs and what were seen by many as strange habits. Before long, some districts began to feel distinctly foreign, with shops selling food the like of which we had never seen. This tendency for foreigners to move in and displace those already living in East London was no new phenomenon; it had already happened at least twice in the preceding 150 years or so. This time though, the newcomers kept on coming and some East Enders found they themselves were the minority in certain streets. This was certainly a novel turn of events and one that created friction.

The French Huguenots had settled in Whitechapel and those already living there had gradually moved outwards. Later, Jewish people from Eastern Europe moved into Whitechapel and displaced the Huguenots. Now, as families from Bengal and Pakistan arrived, the Jewish communities moved west into Ilford and Gants Hill. The way that this current wave of immigration differed from those which had gone before was that whereas the French, the Jews and the Polish seemed to assimilate English society, until they were virtually indistinguishable from anybody else, those coming in the 1960s maintained more of their own, separate identity.

Rivers of Blood and the Dockers

On 20 April 1968, Enoch Powell, a prominent member of Edward Heath's Shadow Cabinet, made a speech in which he warned of the dangers resulting from large-scale immigration. Among other things, he said of ordinary English workers:

For reasons which they could not comprehend, and in pursuance of a decision by default, on which they were never consulted, they found themselves made strangers in their own country. They found their wives unable to obtain hospital beds in childbirth, their children unable to obtain school places, their homes and neighbourhoods changed beyond recognition, their plans and prospects for the future defeated; at work they found that employers hesitated to apply to the immigrant worker the standards of discipline and competence required of the native-born worker.

The speech was denounced as racist and Heath sacked Enoch Powell, although many felt Powell had merely spoken the literal truth, saying publicly what many had noticed but remained silent about. His words touched a chord in the hearts of many East Enders and, three days later, 1,000 London dockers went on strike and marched to Parliament, carrying banners saying 'Back Britain – not black Britain'. The following day, 600 workers at St Katherine's Docks in the East End went on strike in support of Powell. Hundreds of Smithfield porters, many of them East Enders, also marched to Parliament in support of what Enoch Powell had said. However, the changes to the East End by waves of newcomers actually accelerated after 1968.

A Child's View

One might think that growing up against a background of this sort would have made children extremely conscious of race and ethnicity, but I do not believe that this happened at all.

Adults were always raving on about something. If it wasn't the 'coloureds', it was taxes, the cost of food and so on. It was just one of those things which grown-ups got cross about. My Nana went on about all the 'darkies' working at the local hospital; some neighbours were terrified that 'coloureds' would move into the street. It was well-known to these people that once that happened, there went the neighbourhood! There were no black children in my class, but when I did encounter other ethnic groups, I can't recall feeling any of the hostile attitude that I was surrounded by when growing up. The 1960s were a time of change, and immigration was just one more aspect of change. It was clear, even to a child, that the world was going to be a different place than it had been for my parents, or even my older brother, when I grew up.

14

Law and Order

Attitudes to Crime

Growing up in the East End, one naturally acquired a peculiar – one might even say distorted – view of crime. For example, some things which were technically against the law were hardly regarded as being culpable to any degree. Living in such close proximity to the docks, bits and pieces were always finding their way into circulation, usually via some man in a pub. Things 'fell off the back of a lorry' and were sold cheap in the car park of the local pub. I certainly never learned to view the handling or receiving of stolen property in this way as being criminal in any real sense of the word. This is not to say that children growing up in that place and time did not learn the difference between right and wrong; rather that their standards varied a little from those in more affluent areas.

This cavalier attitude to theft applied only to the property of shops and companies. It certainly did not extend to pinching stuff from people's houses. Stealing from your own was regarded as being the lowest type of offence imaginable.

Petty dishonesty was pretty much a backdrop for the lives of East End children. Fiddling fares on the buses and tube was a way of life, as was pinching stuff from shops. The convention was that it was quite acceptable to nick stuff from a shop belonging to a large chain such as Woolworths, but not from the tobacconist at the end of the road. We more or less understood from our parents that taking property from the workplace was, as a rule, OK – always provided, of course, that you weren't caught. This was often viewed as a species of primitive communism; the redistribution of wealth to the masses as an additional reward for their labour. More than once in childhood, I heard some relative talk of something he had stolen from the factory where he worked, describing it as, 'getting some of our own back'. Being 'on the fiddle' was certainly not a pejorative way of describing someone's activities.

It has to be said that this casual acceptance of theft from one's place of employment did, in the long run, rather end up killing the golden goose. In the later 1960s and early '70s, the London Docks were closed down and the whole industry moved to the Essex town of Tilbury. There were a number of reasons for this move to containerisation, but one factor was, without doubt, the enormous amount of cargo which went missing at the London Docks. As a rule of thumb, businesses assumed that ten per cent of any cargo passing through the docks would vanish. They wrote this off as 'shrinkage', but obviously, when somebody came up with a scheme that would eliminate this loss, companies took to it enthusiastically.

Going off now at a slight tangent, it must be pointed out that this tendency to make off with anything that wasn't red-hot or nailed down was not limited to the East Enders working at the docks; it is an unfortunate feature of the British working-man's character that he will often pinch stuff from his place of work whenever he thinks he can get away with it. The modern equivalent of the London Docks is Heathrow Airport, where astonishing quantities of goods go missing all the time; to the extent that the place is know colloquially as 'Thief Row', rather than Heathrow.

I cannot resist at this point an illuminating anecdote. A company filming an historical epic in Spain had made some life-sized and realistic models of dead Roman soldiers. They scattered these around the battlefield scenes and it was a lot cheaper than paying extras to literally lie about all day. They brought half a dozen of these figures back to Britain via Heathrow. When these six life-sized, dead Roman soldier models were unloaded, somebody decided that it would be fine to just leave them propped in a corner for a few hours; no point fussing around to get them locked up safely – who would bother to steal something so utterly useless? Every single one of those figures was pinched within an hour and none were ever recovered. If it's not red-hot or nailed down…

How did this casual and endemic minor dishonesty affect the *mores* of children growing up around the docks? There is in British law a specific criminal offence which is known as 'theft by finding'. This concept would have been literally incomprehensible to any child from the East End throughout the 1960s. The ancient law of 'finders keepers, losers weepers' governed any property or money which should be lost, misplaced or even left untended for too long. The expression 'fell off the back of a lorry' refers to this part of the working-class code of the times. If some item fell off a lorry or horse and cart as it was passing through the streets, then it belonged, as a matter of course, to the first person fortunate enough to come across it or quick enough off the mark to seize it. This is why anybody selling stolen goods in a public house would describe them as having fallen 'off the back of a lorry'; it lent a spurious air of legitimacy to the proceedings. One might hesitate to buy stolen property, but if this or that article really had fallen off the back of a lorry, then it was the finder's property and his to dispose of as he saw fit. Anything found was naturally the rightful property of the first person to claim it. This was simply the morality which children adopted from their elders. We learnt in this way as we got older, the difference between what was regarded as a crime and what was a merely social convention.

I have sometimes wondered if this slightly peculiar and distorted morality which I picked up as a kid was influenced by the origin of the East End itself. English people sometimes make jokes about the Australians being the descendents of thieves, due to the fact that the country was once a penal colony and that transportation there was an alternative to hanging for many offences in the late eighteenth and early nineteenth centuries. Much the same could be said of the East End. Until the middle of the nineteenth century, it was really a rural area, with scattered hamlets and villages stretching into Essex. We can glimpse this long forgotten past in the place names of the East End. Stepney Green, for instance, sounds like a pretty little village.

In the centre of London at that time were a number of places famous for their crowded slums, many of which were full of vagrants and petty criminals. These places were practically no-go areas for the police, who tended to leave the inhabitants to their own devices. Dickens wrote of these slum quarters, which were referred to as rookeries. In *Bleak House* he creates a vivid picture of one such district, which he calls Tom-all-Alone. Some of these rookeries were very ancient, dating back at least as far as the Elizabethan era. A number of them had grown up around ecclesiastical locations which, before the Reformation, possessed a right to sanctuary. Such spots naturally acted as a magnet for vagabonds and rogues of every description! At one time, anybody living here was effectively beyond the reach of the law.

When developers were looking for sites in central London to build the new railway termini, these slum quarters seemed to be the ideal choice for many reasons. It avoided the inconvenience and expense of buying up the property of respectable people, but also promised to rid the greatest city in the world of embarrassing reminders of a less salubrious past. The rookeries were demolished and the huddled masses sheltering within them were sent on their way. They did not get far; most wandered out of London, harried and chivvied along by the police, until they reached the nearest villages outside the city proper – places such as Mile End and Bethnal Green in fact.

Could it be that these shiftless, rag tag wanderers took with them a set of values somewhat at odds with those held by more decent citizens? Is this why 'being on the fiddle' – even the very expression sounds like a bit of Tudor thieves' cant – was never viewed unfavourably in the East End?

From all this has grown a romanticised view of the *mores* of the old East End. Take mugging for instance, especially the mugging of young people. Older inhabitants of East

London shake their heads in disgust upon hearing that in some parts of London today, schoolchildren are regularly targeted by muggers. Such a thing would never, they state with assurance, have happened in the old days. This is quite true, but has nothing at all to do with any real change in morality. It is a purely pragmatic matter. Let us look a little closer at living conditions prevailing in working-class districts of London at a time about which many now grow so nostalgic.

We Could Leave our Doors Open in Those Days

It is perfectly true that until the end of the 1960s it was common practice in the East End to leave back doors open or front doors unlocked. This was a matter of convenience so that children could come and go as they pleased. It is also true that burglary or theft from homes was all but unknown and that the practice of stealing from other people's homes in this way was frowned upon. There was, however, another reason why such thefts were uncommon and it has nothing to do with honesty or community spirit; it was simply that there was nothing worth stealing in the average East End home at that time. These days, an opportunistic thief walking into an ordinary, working-class home in Bethnal Green could swiftly fill a large sports bag with valuable items which can readily be converted to cash. Games consoles, watches, jewellery, iPods, cameras, laptop computers, designer clothing and footwear; the list is endless and growing each year. What would the pickings have been like fifty years ago for a sneak thief in East London?

As it happens, I can remember exactly what the average home at that time contained. The only electrical goods we owned in 1960 were a bakelite radio, which dated from before the Second World War. It was the old sort with valves, which plugged into the mains. That was it; no record player, television or anything else. Roughly half the homes in that part of London in 1960 did not have a television. Even for those which did, the sets themselves were so bulky and cumbersome that it would be impossible for any casual thief simply to make off with one. There were few record players and almost nothing portable which could be sold on for a reasonable amount. In addition to our radio, there were half a dozen books and a few toys. Apart from that were our clothes, but they were hardly worth pinching as most were old and many patched.

This brings us to the mugging of modern children and the real reasons as to why such crimes were unknown fifty years ago. These days, children in East London are regularly robbed on their way to and from school. The situation is so bad in places that special police patrols are mounted to protect them. This is shocking, of course, but in some ways quite understandable. They have with them mobile telephones and iPods and are also likely to be carrying money and to be wearing stylish trainers. All this makes them a natural target for vicious thieves. What possible reason would anybody have had for robbing a schoolboy in 1960? You would have been lucky to gain 6*d* from the business!

One final point needs to be borne in mind when trying to work out how much crime was committed fifty years ago and the extent to which children were the perpetrators or victims of theft and violence. Crime figures rely upon the reporting of offences and until the last few decades, the great majority of theft went unreported to the police. The reason is simple: anybody reporting the theft of a television to the police today does so not because they have any real expectation that police enquiries will lead to the discovery of the thief and restoration of the property. They notify the police in order to get a crime number so that they can claim from their insurance. Because there was little worth pinching in East End homes half a century ago, hardly anybody bothered with household insurance. Anybody coming home and finding that somebody had made off with the wireless would either mark it down to experience or try and track down the thieves themselves. Similarly, if a schoolchild was involved in a scuffle and had his school dinner money taken, it would be very unlikely to end up on the crime statistics for that year! Most parents in the East End would be annoyed with the boy for not fighting back ferociously enough; they certainly would not be dialling 999 to report a mugging.

Considerations of this sort make it extremely hard to work out the actual level of criminal activity in the East End at that time. Quite apart from not needing a crime number for the insurance, there was an almost pathological avoidance of involving the police in day-to-day affairs. Part of this was a desire not to be seen as 'a grass'. If somebody stole from you or assaulted your child, then the easiest way of dealing with the matter was to sort it out for yourself. Calling the police was definitely a last resort, rather than a first response.

One type of theft which was carried out by teenagers did involve other people's houses; even those of neighbours. This was robbing the gas or electric meter. In those days, few people paid a quarterly bill. Instead, they had shilling-in-the-slot meters. Sometimes, fourteen or fifteen-year-olds would take it into their heads to nip into houses, break open these meters and make off with the money. This might typically amount to a couple of pounds; not a fortune, but certainly enough to buy some cigarettes, sweets and a few bottles of pop. This sort of crime was a nuisance because householders were responsible for the meters and answerable for any losses. In other words, if somebody robbed your gas meter, you had to make good the missing money.

Offences of this sort would not end in a police investigation, but the aggrieved party would scour the neighbourhood in search of the thieves. If he found them, he would exact justice and recover as much of his money as had not already been spent in the sweet shop or off-licence.

The Police

As a child, I felt instinctively that the interests of the police were not exactly congruent with those of my family and friends. There was no overt hostility towards the police, but we felt a little wary of them. Many people had some minor piece of illegal activity on the go, in order to make ends meet, and having a police officer poking round the house was something to be avoided if at all possible. Cheeking a policeman was something of a tradition, showing that you were a bit of a lad. I remember clearly the first and only time that I was cheeky in this way.

I was eleven years old and out with some friends near Bethnal Green tube station. A lone police constable on the beat walked towards us, and as we passed I said brightly, 'Wotcher, Dixon,' in reference to the television policeman in

Dixon of Dock Green. Instantly, the officer turned and came up to us, asking who had spoken. I admitted that it was me and he took my name and address, remarking that there was nothing funny about being rude.

I spent the rest of the day with my friends and had completely forgotten about this incident by the time I returned home. My mother greeted me though by asking what I had been doing to make the police come round to the house. This enquiry was accompanied by a clout to my head. It seemed that after leaving me, the policeman had walked round to my house and told my mother about what I had said and warned her that cheekiness of this sort often led to worse things. He advised that if she didn't keep an eye on me, then he and his colleagues would do so. The whole business made a great impression upon me and from that

Carnaby Street in 1968 – the new face of London.

day to this, I do not believe that I have ever treated any police officer with anything other than the greatest courtesy. My Nana, when she heard about it, summed the case up very well, saying, 'Never be funny with a copper!' I have found this to be a sound policy over the last half a century or so!

Despite all this, there was no feeling that the police were actually our enemies. There is a very definite difference between the attitude to the police current among children in that part of London then and now. Today, there is a clear sense of hostility towards the police on the part of many young people, who see them as enemies. For us, things were not at all the same. We were aware that the police might not approve of some of our activities and that if we overstepped the mark, they might take us home and talk to our parents. We even knew that in serious cases, we could be taken to court. None of this made us dislike the police, nor I suspect did they have anything against us really. If I was in serious trouble or lost, I always knew that I could turn to a policeman for help.

Before leaving this subject, I have to make one observation. There might have been the odd piece of cheekiness directed against the police by us kids, but when talking directly to an officer, one would never be anything other than polite and respectful. I do not believe that this was motivated by fear, so much as respect. Two recent incidents show how much the behaviour of children and young people in the East End has changed over the last few decades.

In autumn 2011, there was a report in the paper of a decision by the Court of Appeal. Two police officers had stopped and searched a young man in the East End. He had responded by swearing at them. When they failed to find anything incriminating in his pockets, he told them aggressively, 'I told you f***ing so!' Since he had already been warned about his language, they arrested him for insulting behaviour. There was no dispute around the words which he used; he freely admitted swearing like a trooper. However, Mr Justice Bean ruled that the police should be so used to being sworn at or abused, that it was not an offence for anybody to do so. It emerged that the Metropolitan Police had already instructed officers that they were not to respond if youths swore at them. Youths swearing at a policeman! I simply cannot imagine even the toughest and most devil-may-care of my companions, as teenagers, thinking of such a thing.

In Dalston last week, just round the corner from Ridley Road Market, I witnessed what seemed to me one of the most bizarre spectacles I had ever seen in my life. Two police officers had stopped a young Asian boy; he could not have been more than fifteen. They were asking him questions; I have no idea what it was all about. The boy began to get agitated and raise his voice, and other youths then drifted over to see what was going on. In no time at all, the two officers were being shouted at by a group of young men, none of whom could have been more than seventeen years of age. One boy was literally yelling at the police from a distance of perhaps eighteen inches – so close and so furiously that flecks of spittle were striking them in their faces. Throughout the whole incident, the two policemen remained calm and collected, eventually leaving.

Just imagine being a teenager in the 1960s, shouting and practically spitting in a policeman's face, or using the 'F' word to him. Your feet wouldn't touch the ground; you'd be down the nick that fast. The very thought makes my blood run cold, even at my age; yet this is no isolated event. I have mentioned how fare dodging was very common when I was growing up. If caught, there were two options; either race off at top speed or offer your name and address and apologise profusely. We knew in our hearts that dodging fares was tantamount to stealing and so when we were caught, there was an awareness, even as children, that we had been doing wrong and must wriggle out of it as best we could.

I have seen children and teenagers stopped for this very same thing in the East End over the last few years and have been utterly astonished at the behaviour. Not only are these young people not aware of having done anything wrong, they seem to blame the ticket inspectors or station staff for the situation. I have seen the younger ones glare sullenly and shrug, their sense of grievance palpable. As for the teenagers, they swear and behave in such a menacing fashion that either the police are called or the staff just give up. I have even heard one young man threaten to stab the ticket inspector when he was caught without a ticket!

There is no doubt at all in my mind that the rules and worldview of young people in the East End have undergone a radical change since I was a boy. We might have found the insistence of the police in laying down the law, and seeing that people obeyed it, as a nuisance. Similarly, it was irritating when a bus conductor refused to accept that we had already paid our fare and threatened to throw us off at the next stop. These things were an annoyance, but we did not doubt that moral weight was on their side. Many young people in that same area today seem to become enraged at the slightest suggestion that they should be subject to the same inconvenient conventions as the rest of us.

15

The East End in 1970

At the beginning of this book, I said that memories of the East End from the late 1950s and early '60s tend to be, just like the photographs of that time, in shades of grey. It was a drab, monochrome era. This is in sharp contrast to the late 1960s and early '70s, which somehow blossomed into colour; even if the colours tended to be the bright oranges and muted browns so typical of that period. The modern world had arrived and it was a quantum leap from the gloomy one of the 1950s. Most people in the East End were now living in homes with bathrooms and inside lavatories; a situation which only a generation earlier would have been unthinkable. Although they still lived in the old industrial zone, light years from the West End, those in Bethnal Green and Stepney could not fail to realise that the world had changed radically. Steam trains were a nostalgic memory and colour televisions had arrived; photographs from the time are colourful and bright. The 1960s had changed everything; the old society had somehow crumbled away and been replaced by a new one where ordinary workers could expect to have the same sort of things as the more well off. Standards of living in East London had never been higher.

We have seen that there were also other changes, the full implications of which would not become apparent for another decade or so. The traditional jobs, which boys and girls growing up in the East End had taken for granted, were disappearing. The docks were moving out into Essex, the factories were closing down and the number of vacancies for unskilled workers shrinking rapidly. Within a year or two, the school-leaving age would be raised to sixteen, and instead of the old division between grammar schools and secondary moderns, all children would be attending the same schools; the new comprehensives. The old CSEs, which had been taken by the less academically able at the secondary moderns, were also being abolished. From now on, the dullest working-class child would be expected to study and take the same examinations as those headed for Oxford and Cambridge.

By the 1970s, employers were routinely asking for GCSEs in their advertisements. An illiterate school-leaver might have been able to scrape by in 1959, but things were changing. Education for girls had also become more important. The divorce rate was rising, marriage was taking place at a later age and couples were now living together openly without bothering to get married at all. Working was no longer just something that an East End girl did for a few years after school, before she settled down and became a housewife and mother. It was becoming possible for girls at school in East London to conceive of a future which they could control for themselves, one which did not necessarily even involve marriage and childbearing.

Other changes that took place – the increase in material prosperity to take one example – were no more than reflections of how British society, in general, was adapting at this time; some though were particular to the East End itself. Like so many who grew up in the area, I too have drifted west and live today in a former council house in Debden in Essex, one of the new estates built to accommodate refugees from East London after the war.

16

Childhood in the East End: Separating Myth from Reality

Writing about the experience of childhood in East London fifty years ago is a tricky enterprise, because there is a risk of contradicting or deconstructing not one but two legends which have combined together over the last few years into one enormously powerful mythic narrative. On the one hand is the idea that children at that time may have been poor and lacking in many of the material advantages of young people today, but were far happier, freer and healthier. They played outdoors, free of parental supervision, in perfect safety; there was little traffic to worry about and no chance of being attacked or mugged; their mothers waved them off in the morning, not expecting to see them again until teatime. This vision of a happy and unrestricted childhood is tangled up with the popular image of the East End of half a century ago: a society which was a genuine community, where every member looked out for his or her neighbours and kept an eye on each other's children. Like all legends, there are elements of truth in both these pictures, although in reality the situation was more complex than the popular myth might suggest.

We have seen that children had more freedom in East London fifty years ago than those today can possibly imagine. They roamed the streets from an early age, routinely crossing roads alone from the age of seven or eight. These children did indeed play for many hours at a time out of sight of their parents, unsupervised by any adults. How safe this was for them is certainly open to question. They were far more likely to be knocked down by a car and the fact that so many young children were playing out of doors and crossing roads alone must surely have a bearing upon this sobering fact. By any objective standard, these children were at far greater hazard than children today. They were not only more likely to be killed by cars, but their chances of breaking arms or legs and losing fingers and eyes were vastly higher than is the case today.

The notion that children were, in any sense, healthier fifty years ago is so absurd it hardly needs refutation. This country's infant mortality rate in 1960 was roughly comparable to that of present-day Egypt. The deficiency disease rickets, more commonly associated today with developing countries, was rife, particularly in poorer working-class districts such as the East End. The illness bronchitis was endemic.

What then of the famous 'community' that existed in the East End? Here we find ourselves on very shaky ground, because it is hard to quantify precisely what we mean by 'community'; far harder than comparing sets of statistics relating to infant mortality or the incidence of various diseases. After all, how does one actually measure 'community spirit' or 'looking out for one's neighbour'? There is no objective way in which we may compare today's society with that in a particular part of London in the 1960s. Those of us who grew up in that time and place feel instinctively that people cared more for each other, but how are we to know this for sure?

This brings us to one of the great difficulties when attempting to set out a factual account of the state of society during any writer's childhood. Children do not generally know fully what is going on around them. They do not, as a rule, read the newspapers and are unlikely, in the extreme, to come across infant mortality rates in the *British Medical Journal*. This means that their recollection of events is liable to be skewed and unreliable.

Because there exists no statistical evidence to support the idea of a greater sense of community spirit, we are compelled to fall back on anecdotal evidence which, while it can never be conclusive, may be highly suggestive. Here is one such anecdote; an everyday incident in the East End of the 1960s, which is typical of many. I think that it does indicate a change in behaviour among both adults and children.

I mentioned earlier the way boys used to play by railway lines. On one occasion, when I was twelve, a few friends and I had climbed up the embankment near Stratford station to get onto the line. A passing middle-aged man in an alleyway running by the line spotted us and called for us to come down. There were four of us, ranging in age from twelve to fourteen. He ticked us all off soundly and warned us of the dangers of going near the railway line in this way. I muttered something under my breath, whereupon he booted me up the backside and asked me to repeat what I had said. I declined and he waited until we had all left before continuing his own journey. We did not go back onto the lines that night.

There are several remarkable things about this story. To begin with, this man was a complete stranger. But, nevertheless, he felt that he had a duty to intervene when he saw a group of young people behaving in a way that was hazardous to themselves. He also felt quite justified in inflicting mild corporal punishment. He was also confident that we would accept his authority as an adult and allow him to tick us off and send us about our business. When he told us to come down from the embankment, we came at once. It did not occur to any of us to tell him to clear off and mind his own business.

This trivial example is typical of the attitude of both children and adults at that time. Although we were pretty wild characters, we accepted that this adult had a perfect right to rebuke us. For his part, he knew that we would not fall upon him and threaten to knife him for his sharp words to us. Imagine this happening today! In the first place, the man would not have felt that it was any of his business; he would simply have hurried by and ignored us. Quite apart from any other consideration, any passer-by these days would probably be too scared to challenge a group of youths in this way – anything might happen. And just imagine somebody having the conviction these days to boot a cheeky young boy up the backside! He would soon find himself in court charged with assault.

It is also interesting to think about what our parents' view of the matter would have been, had we ever been foolish enough to tell them about it. I know that they would have felt grateful to the stranger for taking the trouble to speak to us and, in addition, to the boot up my backside, I would have got a clip round the ear from my mother to go with it.

Again, the prevailing attitude today is very different, with parents defiant at any suggestion that their children might be to blame for anything at all.

I have a suspicion that most people who grew up in the East End in those days will have similar stories to tell, of adults who went out of their way to set errant children on the right path, or rescue them from tricky situations. The tendency these days is to rely upon 'the authorities' to tackle other people's children. Thus, with few police officers on the beat and ordinary adults unwilling to intervene, it is all but inevitable that antisocial behaviour should be on the increase.

We regularly read in the newspapers or hear on the news about surveys showing that children today are less physically healthy and more anxious; less psychologically robust or prone to psychiatric problems such as anorexia. This, it is suggested, means that children today are unhappier than they used to be. This may be so, if only we could find some way of measuring happiness and could obtain past data in which precisely the same test had been administered to groups of children in the 1960s. Of course, no such data exist. How could they; fifty years ago, nobody would have thought for a moment to start testing the mental health of children at random in the way which is routinely done these days.

Perhaps if it were possible to conduct such an experiment, we would discover that just as many children in the 1960s felt miserable and depressed, but that instead of being offered counselling, they were told to snap out of it and pull themselves together. There are, without doubt, differences in health between children in the East End of fifty years ago and those who live there today, but it would be hard to say, in some cases, whether those differences meant that things were better or worse now than they used to be.

There is a great deal of concern today about the so-called 'obesity epidemic' which afflicts children in this country. This obesity is especially common among the lower socio-economic groups; in other words, the poorer the family, the more likely are their children to be overweight. Anybody walking round the East End today will certainly see a lot of overweight children, and they often look as though they might, indeed, come from the poorer homes. It is also true that their obesity carries risks of an increased tendency for heart disease, diabetes and various other things liable to shorten lives. Did we see all these overweight children in the East End in the 1960s? No, we did not; therefore children in this part of London are less healthy today than they were fifty years ago. Well yes… and no; but mostly no.

Fifty years ago, there were, indeed, hardly any children with weight problems in the East End; but there were an awful lot of thin ones. In fact, quite a few of them were thin and also suffering from deficiency diseases – diseases that were just as likely to have an unfavourable impact upon their health in later years as obesity is today. Vitamin deficiencies; lack of essential minerals resulting in permanently deformed bones; chronic bronchitis from their living conditions, which would, in many cases, develop in later life into chronic obstructive lung disease.

The more closely we look at the past and try and compare it with the present, the harder we find it to make any claims, with assurance, about which was better or worse. Precisely the same happens when we try to decide whether society in general was better or worse in those days. Perhaps, in

'The Circle of Life'. (Photo by Steve Lewis)

the end, all we can say is that life for children in the East End of the 1960s could be a lot of fun, although there were disadvantages to be living at that time, at least when compared with the way things are today. The idea that the East End was something special, or that childhood then was better than it is today, is impossible to establish one way or another. The most we can say is that life was different then.

Appendix 1

The Origin and Extent of the East End

There exists no official definition of precisely what constitutes the East End. One or two boundaries are generally agreed, although even about those there is debate in some quarters. For example, most would say that the River Thames is the southern limit for the East End and yet there is a school of thought which holds that the inhabitants of Bermondsey in South London are authentic East Enders. This is, however, very much a minority view. It is founded partly upon the fact that Bermondsey is just across the river from the genuine East End and that many residents there worked on the docks just like many East Enders. Perhaps it would help if we examined the history of London and saw how the concept of the East End arose in the first place.

During the nineteenth century, the rookeries and slums of central London were demolished and their inhabitants dispersed in order to make room for the building of the great railway stations such Liverpool Street, Fenchurch

Street, Kings Cross and Euston. Many of the dispossessed moved to the Essex villages and hamlets to the east of the City of London; Mile End, Whitechapel and Stepney. These poverty-stricken refugees of the Industrial Revolution, many of them petty criminals and the rest little better than beggars and vagrants, settled east of London to begin new communities. These origins meant that, from the very beginning, this whole district was a by-word among more respectable citizens for poverty, squalor and crime; a reputation that has proved extraordinarily hard to shake off! The fact is, the forbearers of most of the old East Enders were beggars and petty criminals!

In Whitechapel and parts of Bethnal Green, there was a well-established community of French exiles who made their living from weaving silk. Those who had been uprooted from central London, along with these French artisans, were joined later in the nineteenth century by Irish immigrants and dispossessed Eastern European Jews. These were the people who constituted the nucleus of the East End.

But what was the geographical extent of the area known as the East End? It is generally agreed that the eastern border of the East End is the City of London and that the Thames marks its southerly limit. To the north, parts of the present-day borough of Hackney were recognised to be in the East End; Shoreditch was for instance, but Stamford Hill was probably not. The River Lea marks a convenient boundary to the west, passing as it did through Stratford. Mind you, the Lea is not entirely satisfactory, as it leaves Custom House, Canning Town and Silvertown out of the East End – a preposterous notion to any true East Ender! Most people today would acknowledge the districts of West

Ham and East Ham to be part of the East End, together with Plaistow and Beckton. This is despite the fact that all these parts of London are to the west of the River Lea.

As we saw, there has, over the years, been a drifting west of East Enders into the suburbs and even further out into Essex. For many, the eastern boundary should now be the River Roding rather than the Lea. This would bring into the fold Barking and Manor Park. Some go even further and try to include the northern suburbs of Leyton, Leytonstone and even Walthamstow as being part of the East End.

Ultimately perhaps, the East End is a psychological concept rather than a geographical location. Being an East Ender is a state of mind, independent of precisely which part of East London one was born in. This brings us to another point; the distinction between Cockneys and East Enders. For those outside London, the two expressions are virtually synonymous, but in fact there are important differences (see Appendix 2). The Cockney dialect has always been spread across a far greater area of East London than just the East End. The generally accepted definition of a Cockney is somebody born within the sound of the church bells of Bromley by Bow. Research in the 1970s discovered that on a quiet day, these bells could actually be heard not only across the East End, but as far west as the River Roding. In other words, somebody born in the Essex town of Ilford might, by this criterion, be entitled to call himself a Cockney! Even more disturbingly, the sound of the bells carried across the Thames to parts of South London. Surely those living in Charlton, say, cannot be considered Cockneys?

Appendix 2

The Secret Language of the East End

It may today seem strange to describe Cockney as a 'secret' language. Through the influence of television, elements of Cockney speech have spread far beyond the few square miles of East London, where this distinctive dialect originated. There can be few people in Britain who do not recognise some rhyming slang; for example, 'Use your loaf,' as meaning 'Use your head', (loaf of bread – head). Even senior politicians and younger members of the Royal family now swallow the 'T's' on the ends of words in the traditional Cockney fashion. Right becomes righ' and so on.

Other features of Cockney are, of course, the use of the double negative: 'We don't have none'. Also, the introduction of diphthongs into words which in standard English contain only one syllable: the word 'milk', as spoken in Received Pronunciation, is one syllable; in Cockney it is pronounced as 'me-ork' – two syllables, with no 'L' sound.

So-called 'Estuary English', a watered down version of the Cockney accent, is an accepted way of speaking for many people in South East England. The situation fifty years ago was very different. Cockney English was the dialect – one might almost say language – of a small geographical area between the City of London in the west and the River Roding in the east.

Avoiding Names

Listening to a group of old East Enders talking among themselves fifty years ago would have been a puzzling experience unless you had yourself grown up in the area. This was partly due to the widespread use of rhyming slang and loanwords (see page 180). There was also an almost pathological avoidance of naming people and things. Rather than using given names, the expression 'what's his name', usually abbreviated to 'wasname', was frequently used. Various other ways of referring to individuals without mentioning names might be 'him from across the road', or 'you know, thingy from the brewery'. This tendency became a running joke in the 1980s television series *Minder*, in which George Cole's character would never refer to his wife by her given name, calling her instead 'her indoors'. Inanimate objects were 'watchamacallit', 'thingummybob', 'thingy' or 'whatsitsname'. Whether or not this was a lingering superstitious belief that naming a person or object aloud would render it vulnerable to harm, or because they did not wish to allow any casual listener to divine the precise nature of their business, I never discovered.

I was recently reading Laurie Lee's autobiography, *As I Walked Out one Midsummer Morning*, which is a sequel to

Cider with Rosie. He writes of working on a London building site before the Second World War and describes precisely what I am talking about. Talking of the Cockneys with whom he worked, he says:

> This slang seemed still to be the underworld argot; a secretive and evasive language; and had not, at that time, been elevated into a saloon-bar affectation. When slang was not used, my mates seemed to suffer a curious inhibition, a reluctance to name people and things: ''ere, what's-yer-name, mate. Chuck us over that what-d'ya-call-it, will yer? Got to make a what's-it fer this thingummy-jig.' I don't think it was laziness or lack of vocabulary, but rather an instinctive concealment which giving names might betray.

This is exactly how I remember older people talking. Combined with truncated rhyming slang, this would give rise to sentences such as, 'Old wasname from across the road fell right bang on his aris.' The end result was sentences that nobody living outside East London could hope to decode. This brings us neatly to the question of rhyming slang, an exclusively Cockney trick of speech.

Rhyming Slang

Most people are vaguely aware that Cockney rhyming slang involved the use of replacing words with phrases where the final word rhymes with the word which one wishes to avoid using plainly. 'Look' becomes 'butcher's hook'; 'stairs' become 'apples and pears', and so on. The phrase is then truncated to the first word, which does not rhyme at all with the word one wishes to use. So we use 'butcher's' – as in 'let's have a butcher's' – to mean 'look'. As remarked earlier, some of these shortened expressions have now passed into general usage. Many people refer to feet as 'plates', without considering the derivation from 'plates of meat'.

The situation becomes more complicated when double rhyming and truncation is used further to obscure the original word. The use of 'aris' is a perfect example of this. Rhyming slang for 'arse' was, at one time, 'bottle and glass'. This became shortened, or truncated, to 'bottle'. This word was then itself replaced with 'Aristotle', or 'aris' for short. Later still, 'aris' itself was replaced by 'plaster of Paris'. This constant mutation meant that words could change in a matter of months and no outsider could hope to keep track of the new usage unless he was actually living and working in East London.

Loanwords

Mixed in with the rhyming slang were many loanwords from other languages. Cockney has always acquired foreign words easily and the more obscure the better. This too was part of the same apparent reluctance to talk plainly. It certainly acted to exclude outsiders. Many of the words used by Cockneys were picked up during army service in other parts of the world. These days, although one does encounter soldiers from time to time, it is something of a rarity to come across a man who has served in the armed forces. When I was a child, everybody's father had been in the army during the Second World War, and their grandfathers had also been soldiers in the First World War.

The same went for uncles. Nearly every male relative over the age of forty had been in the army.

A consequence of all this travel while in the army, to places like India and the Middle East, was that various Arabic and Hindi expressions were added to the Cockney vocabulary. In addition to using the word 'butcher's', to signify having a look at something, we had 'shufti', from Arabic and 'dekko' from Urdu. There were two practical consequences of having so many words all with a similar meaning. The first was, of course, that outsiders would struggle to follow what was being said. The second was to give Cockney speech a richness and ability for nuance that was unrivalled in standard English.

To have 'a butcher's' meant simply to look at something. Having 'a dekko', from the Urdu dheko (imperative form of 'look'), indicated speed; a dekko was a quick glance. 'A shufti', on the other hand, had connotations of a reconnaissance mission. To have a shufti suggested that you were in some way spying out the land. The curious thing is that although many middle-class men also served in the armed forces during the two world wars, as well as many working-class men from the provinces, I have never encountered anybody but a Cockney who habitually used these words.

Another source of Cockney vocabulary was the languages of minority ethnic groups in this country; chiefly Jewish people and Gypsies. Quite a few of the words which we think of as being typically Cockney actually have their origins in Romany or Yiddish. There could hardly be a more Cockney word than 'mush', as in 'Oy mush, I'm talking to you!' This word is all but identical to the Romany word for 'man'. 'Pal' comes from the Romany for 'brother' and 'shiv' (meaning a knife used as a weapon) is cognate with the Romany *chiv*, meaning 'blade'. Yiddish gives us 'nosh' for food.

The effect of combining the truncated rhyming slang with various foreign words, swallowing all the medial and terminal 'T's' in a sentence and adding diphthongs to monosyllabic words was to render the ordinary speech of Cockneys utterly incomprehensible to any but those born and brought up in East London.

Let's look at the sort of typical, short sentence which Cockneys once used all the time and analyse it. I shall use apostrophes to indicate glottal stops; the gulping omission of the 'Ts' in the middle of or at the end of words. Here is a genuine example of old Cockney, in this case addressed to me, as a grubby ten-year-old who had just come from playing on a bombsite, by my Nana: 'Gor, sta' er your bo'.'

Now, looked at objectively in this way, we might almost be dealing with a transliteration of a phrase from a foreign language. Yet the meaning is perfectly plain to those who were raised in this culture. 'Gor', 'cor' or 'coo' are all Cockney shunt words, used as euphemisms to avoid taking the Lord's name in vain. That most traditional of Cockney phrases, 'Cor blimey!' belongs to the same family. To any old-time East Ender, 'gor' would be understood immediately to be a contraction of 'Gor blimey!' or 'Gor strewth!' These are both abbreviations themselves of magnificent, Shakespearean oaths – 'God blind me!' and 'God's truth!' The East London expression 'lumme' is derived in the same way from 'God love me!'

What then are we to make of the rest of the sentence: 'sta' er your bo'?' Written in full, with the missing 'Ts' replaced, this would be, 'the state of your boat'. Even now, we are no better advanced. What is this boat to which my grandmother was referring? Easy, this is no more than another of those pieces of truncated rhyming slang at which we looked earlier. Boat is short for boat race, rhyming slang for 'face'. And so the sentence written out in standard English, would read, 'May God blind me; just look at the state of your face!'

So difficult was Cockney to understand for those who were not from a relatively small area of London, that a case could perhaps be made for regarding it if not as a separate language, then at the very least as a creole; similar to but separate from English.

In addition to the rhyming slang and foreign loanwords were other expressions, the derivation of some of which is wholly obscure. A single word may be used in very different senses depending entirely upon context. Take the case of a man who announces that he needs a 'pony'. This can be a reference to a desire to defecate (pony and trap meaning 'crap' in rhyming slang), or he could equally well be expressing his need for £25. There are a number of specific words for various sums of money in Cockney. Pony means £25, a monkey is £500 and a ton is £100. Incidentally, by the kind of double-rhyming slang which was discussed above, the slang for excrement became 'macaroni'; 'crap' became 'pony and trap'; 'pony and trap' was abbreviated to 'pony'; and the word 'macaroni' gradually replaced 'pony'.

Cockney preserves many ancient expressions, even though they might be corrupted and mispronounced. I mentioned the case above of 'Gor blimey!' as being a corruption on 'May God blind me'. The traditional Cockney greeting of 'wotcher' has similarly archaic origins. No lesser person than Dr Johnson was irritated by hearing Londoners from the east of the city hailing each other in this way; he called 'wotcher' a ludicrous word. So what does it actually mean?

'Wotcher' is an abbreviation of the medieval greeting 'what cheer?' The earliest written record of this expression dates from 1440. The use of the word 'cheers' in the East End, used to signify thanks, has the same derivation.

The Spread of Cockney

At one time, hardly anybody outside East London would have been able to make neither head nor tail of an awful lot of the day-to-day speech used by Cockneys. Television and radio have changed this dramatically. Programmes like *Steptoe and Son* in the 1960s made a point of using working-class London expressions and these became commonly used in other parts of the country. Before this happened, some of those working in broadcasting used the general ignorance of rhyming slang to play jokes on their employers and use dubious expressions on air. *The Goon Show* was an early example of this kind of thing in the 1950s.

Spike Milligan played various characters in *The Goon Show*, including Eccles and Moriarty. He also devised a new character, an army officer called Captain Hugh Jampton. This looks fine in print and nobody at the BBC thought anything of it. The joke became apparent to Cockney listeners when Milligan began slurring the pronunciation of this name. According to the script, Milligan was saying things like, 'This is Hugh Jampton, on top of St Paul's Cathedral.' Nothing in the least objectionable about that, just a roving reporter signing off to his listeners. However, the way that Milligan pronounced the lines was heard by Cockney listeners as, 'This is huge 'ampton on top of St Paul's Cathedral.' 'Hampton' is, of course, a truncated form of the rhyming slang for 'prick' – Hampton Wick!

Appendix 3

A Walk Around the Old East End

It is hard today to recapture the atmosphere of the East End as it once was. Nevertheless, there are a few small areas which have remained virtually unchanged over the last century or so. The streets surrounding Columbia Road Market, for example, are typical of how so much of this part of London once looked. Poky little two-up two-downs with the front doors opening directly onto the pavement, telegraph poles supporting sagging wires, cast-iron lampposts, even cobbled roads in some places. Poking around behind some of these houses reveals other places which have somehow remained unchanged. Among these are narrow, cobbled lanes no more than 10ft wide which would not look out of place in a Cornish fishing village.

Here is a short walk which gives something of the flavour of the East End as it once was. Take the Central Line tube to Bethnal Green and then walk from there down Bethnal Green Road. You will come to a little turning on the left called Viaduct Street. If you walk down this, you will come to a large grassy area called Weavers Fields. On your left is an adventure playground. The walkways and climbing frames here are brightly painted, but all play is supervised and controlled by play leaders. This adventure playground actually stands on an old bombsite, where the children of the East End once played freely. Keep walking into Weavers Fields. Ahead of you is an old Victorian school; almost all that now remains of the buildings which once stood here. The alleyways and streets were not destroyed by the Blitz though. Indeed, they survived the war almost intact. There were rows of terraced houses and little cottages, some of which dated from the eighteenth century. Around 1960, the local authority decided to knock the whole lot down and relocate the occupants in the blocks of flats that you see around you. To judge whether or not this was an improvement, turn right and walk over to the row of houses in Derbyshire Street, which faces onto Weavers Green. I wonder which most people would rather live in; one of these houses or one of the flats in the nearby blocks?

The old Victorian school on Weavers Fields.

A Victorian school near Columbia Road.

Keep walking along Derbyshire Street, keeping Weavers Fields on your left. You will come to a pub on the left and then Hereford Street. Turn left here and then left again at the end of the street. On your left you will find a Victorian building; a former Bath House. Most houses around here lacked bathrooms and one either used a tin bath in front of the fire or came here for a bath.

Retrace your steps along Hereford Street and keep heading north along Buckfast Street. On the right is what must surely be the narrowest street in London. It is marked in the A to Z as Voss Street, but it is a cobbled lane no more than 10ft wide. When you reach the main road, turn left and cross over. The first turning on the left is Squirries Street. Carry on and this becomes Durant Street. Turn left into Wellington Row. On the right are terraced houses of the sort which once made up most of the housing in this district and, indeed, the East End in general. On the opposite side of the street are new blocks of low-rise flats.

Keep walking until you come to a turning on the right called Barnet Grove. From now on, we must start looking above street level. At one time, there were pubs and corner shops at the end of practically all these little streets. As you turn right into Barnet Grove, look at the buildings on both sides of the road. They are two Victorian pubs, separated by only 20ft or so. Both are now private houses. One was called The Prince of Wales and the other Queen Victoria. Their names are still visible in the stucco at the tops of the buildings.

As you walk down Barnet Grove, look at the street corners that you pass. The moulding tells you that there were

The former Bath House near Weavers Fields.

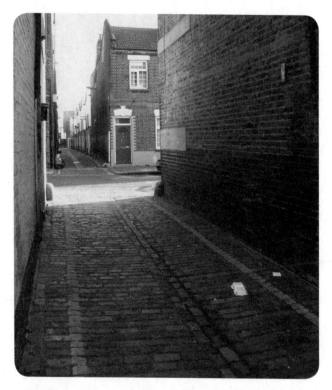

Voss Street.

once shops on the corners of all these streets. Look down Quilter Street as you pass; this is what the whole area once looked like. Just before we reach Columbia Road, there is a complete old shop on the left-hand side. It is very dilapidated and in need of painting, but this is typical of the sort of shops found all over East London in the 1960s. The window frames and door are made of wood and instead of huge expanses of

A local shop would have been here on the street corner.

plate glass, there are small panes of ordinary window glass. The streets here are well worth investigating; the whole area is like a time capsule.

When you come to Columbia Road, turn left. A little way along is a tiny cobbled street called Ezra Street. Walk down here and you might as well be in the nineteenth century.

These streets around Columbia Road are the best-preserved area of the East End as it once was, but there are other fragments which still survive. Beck Road, which runs from Mare Street in Hackney to Sheep Lane, has remained unchanged since the 1930s. It is sometimes used for films set before the Second World War. These terraced houses have their front doors opening straight onto the pavement and a railway viaduct cutting across the street. Further

The cobbled alley near Ezra Street.

Beck Road, a survivor from the old East End.

towards the city, there are even stranger survivals, including the oldest shop in London; a perfectly preserved early eighteenth-century shop front in Artillery Street, a stone's throw from Petticoat Lane.

It is true that much work needed to be done on the remaining old houses in the East End, to make them habitable according to twentieth and twenty-first-century standards. To me, these brick streets, though, are infinitely more appealing than the concrete blocks which replaced them. If you continue walking along Columbia Road, you will reach Shoreditch, where a bus will take you south to Liverpool Street station.

A walk through the backstreets will bring the past to life more vividly than any amount of print. For those like me, who grew up in the East End of London of half a century ago, a stroll like this will recreate a world which has almost vanished for good.